More praise for *Funeral Home Customer Service A-Z*

"This is the definitive guide to consistently delivering extraordinary customer service. It is an excellent training tool and reference guide for new and experienced staff."

John J. Horan, Horan & McConaty Funeral Service/Cremation, Colorado

"Alan Wolfelt has created an excellent road map for funeral professionals wishing to move beyond good services to positive funeral Experiences for client families."

Beacham McDougald, McDougald Funeral Home and Crematorium, North Carolina

"Our firm has consulted with Alan Wolfelt for more than a decade and we have seen firsthand his dedication to helping funeral directors better meet the needs of hurting families. This amazing book is a must-read for everyone connected to funeral service."

Paul Fletcher, Turner & Porter Funeral Homes, Ontario

"Now is the time funeral directors must believe in the importance of the work they do for grieving families and the communities they serve. Funeral Home Customer Service A-Z *will inspire your passion and teach you the skills necessary to carry out our mission of compassionate and meaningful service."*

John C. Carmon, former President, NFDA

Funeral Home Customer Service A-Z

Funeral Home Customer Service A-Z

Creating Exceptional Experiences
for Today's Families

Alan D. Wolfelt, Ph.D.

Companion
PRESS

An imprint of the
Center for Loss and Life Transition

Fort Collins, Colorado

FSC

© 2004 by Alan D. Wolfelt, Ph.D.

Companion Press is an imprint of the Center for Loss and Life Transition, 3735 Broken Bow Road, Fort Collins, Colorado 80526, (970) 226-6050, www.centerforloss.com.

Companion Press books may be purchased in bulk for sales promotions, premiums and fundraisers. Please contact the publisher at the above address for more information.

Printed in the United States of America.

13 12 11 10 09 08 07 06 05 04   5 4 3 2 1

ISBN 1-879651-44-0

*To my hundreds of funeral director friends across North America,
who have inspired me to contribute to funeral service education,
and in memory of my father, Don Wolfelt, who taught me
early in life about compassion, perserverance, integrity
and service to God and my fellow human beings.*

Also by Alan Wolfelt

Creating Meaningful Funeral Experiences: A Guide for Caregivers

Creating Meaningful Funeral Ceremonies: A Guide for Families

Death and Grief: A Guide for Clergy

Interpersonal Skills Training: A Handbook for Funeral Home Staffs

The Journey Through Grief: Reflections on Healing

Understanding Your Grief: Ten Esential Touchstones for Finding Hope and Healing Your Heart

Companion Press is dedicated to the education and support of both the bereaved and bereavement caregivers. We believe that those who companion the bereaved by walking with them as they journey in grief have a wondrous opportunity: to help others embrace and grow through grief—and to lead fuller, more deeply-lived lives themselves because of this important ministry.

For a complete catalog and ordering information, write or call or visit our website:

Companion Press
The Center for Loss and Life Transition
3735 Broken Bow Road
Fort Collins, CO 80526
(970) 226-6050
FAX 1-800-922-6051
wolfelt@centerforloss.com
www.centerforloss.com

Contents

"A customer is the most important visitor on our premises. He is not dependent on us. We are dependent on him. He is not an interruption of our work. He is the purpose of it. He is not an outsider to our business. He is part of it. We are not doing him a favour by serving him. He is doing us a favour by giving us the opportunity to do so."

—Mahatma Gandhi

Preface

Funeral Home Customer Service A-Z is for those of you in funeral service who are concerned about your future as well as that of the profession. We need to raise awareness that creating exceptional funeral Experiences is an ongoing, all-the-time issue, not a sometimes issue.

This book is for those of you in funeral service who recognize that change is positive. This book is for those of you in funeral service I refer to as strivers. The malcontents, if you will. Strivers constantly seek to improve the value of both the service and the products they offer the families they are honored to serve. If ever there was a time for strivers in funeral service, it is now!

This book is for those of you in funeral service I refer to as "strivers."

Every day you have the opportunity to distinguish your funeral home from others by providing fantastic service to the families of your community. Through sensitive, compassionate and caring service, you and those you work with can demonstrate the unique value that your funeral home provides and reinforce in the minds and hearts of those you serve that they made the right decision in coming to you.

This book is for those of you in funeral service who recognize that new consumer attitudes and values about funeral service are requiring you to do things differently than in the past and to be more creative and open to new ideas that families bring you. But this is not all bad; in fact, it is good, because it creates opportunities for you to change with or ahead of your new customer.

This book is for those of you in funeral service who want to create a value-added service culture in your funeral home—a culture in which everyone in the funeral home feels and acts accountable for satisfying (and surprising) families. This book is for owners and managers to read, internalize, and distribute to every employee as a handbook on delivering fantastic customer service.

Perhaps most important, this book is for anyone who works in a funeral home who really wants to make a difference. It's for anyone who is passionate about raising the level of customer service and creating meaningful funeral Experiences in his or her funeral home.

In this book, I'm expressing a customer service philosophy and practice developed over the last 25 years of involvement as an author and educator in funeral service. While some might perceive me as an "outsider," I want you to know that I lived and worked in a progressive funeral home for more than eight years. Today I work with funeral homes across North America and enjoy writing the column "Customer Care" for *The Director*, your major trade journal in funeral service. My Canadian friends in funeral service are familiar with a similar column I pen for *Canadian Funeral News*. I'm proud to be perceived by many as a "change-agent" within funeral service. I am passionate about helping funeral home personnel be the best that they can be.

I wrote this book with several guiding principles in mind: practicality, simplicity, and effectiveness. First, this book must make sense to everyone in the funeral home—not just owners and managers. My hope is that any person on staff can pick up this book and say, "I can identify with that and make use of this information," and then feel motivated to do it. Second, the ideas in this book must be able to be implemented and made use of. And finally, this book must make a difference in creating unique, meaningful, memorable funeral Experiences for the families you serve.

The book is organized in two parts. Part One explains the trends impacting funeral service today, the needs of the "new customer," and the implications of the advent of the Experience Economy for funeral service. Part Two is the A-Z section—the alphabetical walk through practical customer service subtopics, from A for Aftercare to C for Cremation to P for Promptness to V for Visitation to ZZZzzzzz for, well, you'll see.

Throughout the book, I've included real-world examples and advice from visionary funeral homes and directors across North America. Their practices and philosophies reveal them to be journeymen Experience-makers—braving the sometimes choppy waters of the Experience Economy as we speak. I'm sure you will join me in thanking them for freely sharing their ideas and wisdom.

I invite you to first read Part One of *Funeral Home Customer Service A-Z* with care, for only after you've considered what I have to say about creating funeral Experiences with a capital E will the ideas in Part Two really resonate. Then dip in and out of Part Two as you see fit, reading those alphabetical snippets that most interest you and saving the rest for a rainy (or rotten customer service) day.

Ultimately, my hope is that you share with me the belief that for funeral service to survive and thrive into the future, that everyone involved (from owners and managers to part-time staff) must: 1) Be open to reminders of long-established customer service skills; and 2) Constantly strive to creatively develop new customer service skills.

I also hope that you are reading this book because you believe in the value of funeral service. I hope you are reading this book because you are proud to be a service provider to people who come to you at one of life's most difficult times. And, I hope you are reading this book because you are an open learner.

In the words of Eric Hoffler, "In a time of drastic change, it is the learners who inherit the future. The learned find themselves equipped only to live in a world that no longer exists."

Good luck, and happy learning!

Alan D. Wolfelt

Chapter One

Boiled Frogs and Other Phenomena

A frog placed in a pan of boiling water simply jumps out, saving itself.

But a frog dropped into cool water that is then gradually brought to a boil does not jump out. Instead, it enjoys the water's initial warmth and seems to be unaware of the rising temperature. As the heat increases, the frog becomes disoriented and eventually boils to death.

Is your funeral home saving itself or are you boiling to death?

Like the cool water that is gradually brought to a boil, funeral service is changing, slowly but surely. If your funeral home is not consciously and proactively registering and responding to these incremental changes, you will surely suffer the same fate as our amphibious friend.

Is your funeral home saving itself or are you boiling to death?

The good news is that saving yourself from the simmering waters of funeral service is as simple as providing dynamic customer service that results in exceptional funeral Experiences for families. Any funeral home that puts its mind and applies its heart to this task is up to the challenge.

The Service Crisis Challenge

First, let me acknowledge that the majority of funeral directors—owners, managers and frontline personnel alike—genuinely want to deliver exceptional customer service. Across all of funeral service, in both small and large funeral homes, family-owned and corporate, most people truly believe that the "customer is king." However, close observation of funeral service suggests that there is often a gap between the desire to offer excellent service and the performance of that service.

Here are a few of the reasons for this phenomenon:

• *The Customer Has Changed*

The consumer-focused movement that began in the 1960s dramatically changed people's expectations of business throughout North America. The government responded to the Ralph Nader advocates and created new consumer protection laws, such as the FTC's Funeral Rule. The politics of consumer protection raised people's paranoia that they might be ripped off and increased their general service expectations as well.

Today's consumers are better-educated. They want value for their money and aren't afraid to ask for explanations of charges. Nor are they afraid to comparison shop. In fact, for some people today there is more cachet in saving money on funeral services than there is in spending a lot of money.

In addition to being more savvy shoppers, today's funeral home customers have also been influenced by our mourning-avoiding, efficiency-based culture. To paraphrase these social influences, "I don't want to hurt and the funeral makes me acknowledge pain. Besides, faster is better." Many, though certainly not all, primary survivors lack an understanding of the value of ritual and downplay their need to mourn the death.

You may have also heard it said that the new customers "don't always know what they want, but they do know what they don't want." They don't understand funerals and they need funeral care providers who will simplify and demystify the process for them.

See Chapter 2 for more on the new customer.

• *The Death of the Product Solution*

Today, funeral service is much less product-driven than it has historically been. In the past, the customer was more interested in the casket. Today's funeral director must consciously work to create a package of *experiences* to offer families in conjuction with—or even instead of—the product. To survive into the future, funeral service must focus on being customer- and experience-driven, not product-driven. After all, the same casket can usually be provided by different funeral care providers or casket merchandisers and accessed via the Internet. The difference between one funeral home and another has increasingly become the package of experiences that come with the product.

• *Management Philosophies Have Resisted Change*

Today's new customer requires a new management philosophy. While some funeral homes have adapted more contemporary management methods, many are still operating on a dated model. Consider the ways in which a 1950s management model vs. a 2000s management model might respond to various customer service challenges:

CHALLENGE	1950'S MODEL	2000'S MODEL
Requirements of Family Served	Assume requirements are met. 75% of families wanted the same thing (traditional funerals)	Constantly research requirements and change as appropriate
Level of Service Priority	Nice to have good service and assume it is provided	Major priority of management. Constantly train staff to focus on excellent service and the creation of meaningful Experiences.
Communication Patterns Among Staff	Top down, directive style of management. Employee feels fortunate to have a job	Interactive, bottom up style of management. Employee is seen as an internal customer of management.
Measurement of Quality of Service Delivered	Families served tell us we did a good job, high level of service quality assumed.	Customer-centered goals are created and continually measured.

In short, today's funeral home managers must *actively* promote excellence in customer service if they are to keep in step with contemporary management philosophies. Funeral homes that fall back on the status quo will find themselves falling behind in market share.

Several years ago, George Land wrote an interesting book entitled *Grow or Die*. In his book he proposed a growth model for how organizations and markets change. You may be familiar with a number of change models, but I think Land's best applies to contemporary funeral service.

In his model there are three phases of growth:

Phase I: Formative
Phase II: Normative
Phase III: Integrative

In the first phase, also called the formative phase, the business or profession is just starting up. Think of today's dot-com companies. Formative businesses either find a successful pattern or close up shop. In its formative phase, characterized by small, family-run funeral homes, funeral service indeed found a successful pattern and continued on to Phase II.

The normative phase is a period of high productivity and profitability because the success pattern has been identified and is being replicated efficiently. Certainly during the first three-quarters of the 1900s, funeral service enjoyed the benefits of this normative phase.

But at some point in late Phase II, the business or profession hits the proverbial wall. They have grown as much as they can using the old success pattern. Markets change, growth in profitability and market share flattens and the search for new solutions begins. The call for changing the basic business and services strategies grows loud and strong. At the same time, the customer often changes.

Funeral service saw the rumblings of late Phase II as early as the 1970s. Customers began to ask for cremation. Low pricing and cremation began to be marketed in tandem. Cremation societies and direct disposition specialists emerged. The funeral home consolidation trend also began. Preneed sales re-emerged (it was first popular in the 1930s, during the Depression) as a marketing focus. Boomers began to come of age. The customer changed and the market changed.

The business of the past is not, and cannot be, the business of the future.

Funeral service now finds itself in Phase III, the Integrative phase, which calls for a contemporary management philosophy. The question facing many in funeral service is: Will you thrive in Phase III, or will you slowly drift away, close down or sell out (an option less attractive and viable than it was 15, 10 and even 5 years ago, when independents sold out for big money to consolidators, who have since struggled to survive)?

The business of the past is not, and cannot be, the business of the future. But there is a future in funeral service. And for funeral homes that heed the demands of the Boomer generation and experience economy, that future is both exciting and bright.

• The Importance of Employee Training Has Been Overlooked

Without ongoing training, owners, managers, and employees will not provide top-notch customer service. Everyone benefits from being exposed to new skills, attitudes, concepts and ideas.

While mortuary colleges have made strides in teaching customer service skills, the bulk of the educational experience is still on embalming and preparation. Employers should not assume that the new graduate is qualified to fulfill the customer service obligations of the position.

My experience suggests that many funeral homes place little, if any, emphasis on ongoing staff training. The potential result can be a downward service spiral. One unhappy, untrained employee can result in many unhappy customers. The more the customer is unhappy, the more the staff is unhappy, and so the cycle continues.

One negative interaction between a staff member and the family being served can cause headaches; that small incident can overshadow all of the good things. This fact alone underlines the importance of ongoing customer service training for every funeral home employee, from the funeral director to the part-time assistant.

• The Evolution of the Large Corporate Structure

Of today's 23,000 funeral homes across the United States, about 20% are owned and managed by large corporations. It is common knowledge that many of these have been struggling with disappearing profit margins (and in some cases, bankruptcy). As an organization grows, it tends to drift away from the needs of the frontline customer. Sometimes it is tempting for the corporate executive to increase prices to enhance cash flow while downplaying the need for an ongoing focus on customer service excellence.

Corporate growth may also lead executives into focusing more on the convenience and needs of the organization than on its customers. Even well-trained frontline employees cannot overcome the problems of rigid systems, foolish rules, and cost-driven policies that might create customer service glitches.

As the corporate hierarchy grows and policymakers become more distant from customers, the risk is that people in the system may forget who the customers are. Though this is certainly not true of all corporations in funeral service, I have observed that it has happened to some of the major players. To their credit, they are now making an effort to focus more on the needs of families served.

The challenge for funeral service corporations small and large is to keep their ears to the ground and listen to what the customer, on the local level, is telling them. Bottom-up management techniques facilitate this process. In large part, the question is: Can these corporations reinvent their corporate culture, from being acquisitions-focused to operations-focused companies? At present, the jury is out on this one. It would seem that independents are better positioned to create Experiences.

Developing a Service Strategy

Developing a service strategy involves defining your potential customers, discerning their expectations and matching their expectations with your ability to deliver service (see Planning). Operating a funeral home without a defined service strategy may have worked 25 years ago, but it won't work today. Without such a strategy, you don't know who your customers are and how much they value different aspects of the products, services and experiences you provide.

Funeral homes across North America must realize that this service crisis affects them all.

Owners, managers, and frontline employees must realize that customer service excellence is a strategic process. Lipservice, slogans on stationery and advertisements won't suffice in today's world. Families served and those you hope to serve must be at the center of all your management decisions, changed attitudes and customer-friendly behaviors.

Moreover, funeral homes across North America must realize that this service crisis affects them all. Funeral homes in small communities sometimes think that customer service problems only apply to large funeral homes in large cities. This is simply not true. If it hasn't already, the service crisis will soon reach even the smallest of funeral homes.

So who are your customers and what do they want? They bear little resemblance to your customers of past generations, that's for sure. They're skeptical, they're surly and again, they don't always know what they want, but they do know what they don't want. They're Boomers and they're taking the world of funeral service by storm. Let's get to know them a little bit better.

Chapter Two

The New Customer: Boomers and Beyond

It has been said that funeral service is one of the few recession-proof businesses. At this writing, about 2.3 million Americans die per year. This figure is expected to remain relatively constant until the year 2010, at which time the number of deaths will swell as the first wave of the Baby Boomer generation reaches life expectancy.

Do these statistics foretell a bright future for funeral service?

Yes and no. While demographics do guarantee future numbers (how many industries can say that?), Boomers are a new and very different customer of funeral services. Understanding their wants and needs and then tailoring services to not only meet but exceed those needs is increasingly essential for funeral homes. Conversely, failing to truly serve Boomers (and their progeny, Generations X & Y, after them) will be the downfall of many funeral homes.

A couple of years ago, Batesville Casket Company commissioned a national telephone study,* talking with more than 800 consumers 40 and older. Their objective was to better understand consumers' attitudes and beliefs about funerals and funeral products. Under the assumption that a generation's experience of growing up in the same era collectively shapes their thinking, attitudes and behavior, Batesville smartly chose to analyze data from a generational perspective rather than breaking out respondents by gender, income or education.

Batesville's study looked at "GI Generation" consumers, born 1901-1924; "Silent Generation" consumers, born 1925-1942; and Boomers, born 1943-1964. Of the three groups, they found Boomers to be much less satisfied with the funerals they had been a part of. They were also dissatisfied with the arrangement process, wanting more information, more time to make the arrangements and more ideas for personalizing the service. Finally, Boomers didn't value the casket nearly as highly.

Coupled with these findings about Boomer predilections is the fact that Boomers don't attend many funerals. According to the 2000 Wirthlin Group survey, on average people attend less than one funeral per year, down from 1.5 funerals per year just 10 years ago. Nearly one-in-three 30-year-olds haven't been to a funeral in the last two years. Boomers are not accustomed to making funeral arrangements and haven't attended many services. Naturally, this means they are often not aware of the value of funerals.

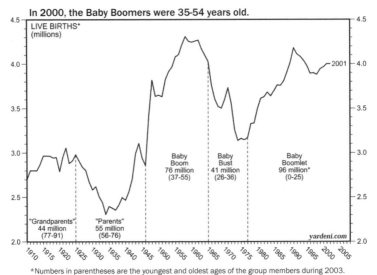

*Numbers in parentheses are the youngest and oldest ages of the group members during 2003.

And then there's the concomitant upswing in cremation rates.

The Cremation Association of North America reports that in 1999, 25% of all the people who died in the U.S. were cremated, skyrocketing from the 1962 figure of 3.61%. The same organization projects the cremation rate will surpass 40% by the year 2010, and climb to 50% by the year 2021.

However, the use of cremation in the U.S. varies greatly by region. For example, states with 1999 rates higher than 50% included Hawaii, Washington, Nevada, Oregon and Montana. On the opposite end of the spectrum were Alabama, Mississippi, West Virginia, Tennessee and Kentucky—all with cremation rates at 7% or less. Nonetheless, even these states with lower cremation rates saw 2-4% increases from 1992-1999.

In Canada, 42% of all the people who died in 1998 were cremated, up from 36% in 1994. This figure is projected to rise to 47% in 2010. As in the U.S., however, Canadian cremation rates vary by province—just over 73% of British Columbian's were cremated in 1998 versus 19% of New Brunswick residents— but continues to rise overall.

The latest Wirthlin Group report tells us that proponents of cremation are generally white, younger than 55 (Boomers), in a higher income bracket, better educated and do not own a cemetery property. Why are Boomers increasingly choosing cremation? Again, the Wirthlin Group Report reveals that 24% choose cremation because it's less expensive, 17% for environmental considerations, 13% because it's "simpler, less emotional and more convenient," 11% because it's their "preference," and 7% because they don't like the thought of the body being in the earth.

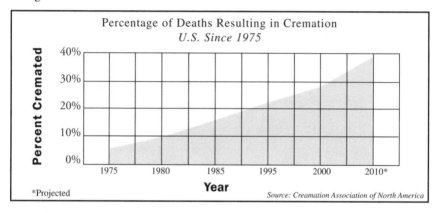

Percentage of Deaths Resulting in Cremation
U.S. Since 1975

*Projected · **Year** · Source: Creamation Association of North America

Fortunately, Boomers also see cremation and funeral or memorial services as going hand-in-hand. About 80% of those who would choose cremation for themselves would like some sort of accompanying service: 32% would prefer a traditional service; 23% would opt for a private service; and 25% would choose a memorial service.

So we know that Boomers are not very familiar with funerals. They come to the arrangement table somewhat skeptical of traditional funerals, though they most often would like some sort of service. They don't care as much about the casket and indeed, are more likely to choose cremation for body disposition. Instead of concerning themselves with the casket, they want more information about the entire funeral process and more ideas for personalizing the service.

And We Wonder Why Boomers Question the Need for Traditional Funerals

Despite these trends, despite the fact that day after day Joe and Jill Boomer are walking into every funeral home across North America, some people in funeral service still seem genuinely shocked and dismayed that the public is questioning the way things are done. But we *have* to have funerals and funeral homes, they protest. It's always been done this way! People die and we have time-honored ways of handling this transition!

A testament to the fact that Boomers want personal services...
Houston Chronicle
Monday, April 20, 1998

Deaths

In Memory of
JOY F. McCLOSKY

April 4, 1931   April 20, 1993

I'd like to take this opportunity to thank everyone who grieved with us when we lost her 5 years ago, and **apologize for the "generic" funeral we had for her.** In my state of shock and grief **I made a very bad choice with her funeral and the lack of appropriate eulogy.** I'd like to try, in a small way, to make up for it now. She was such a special person that I really don't know the right words to truly express how I feel. All I can say is there is a hole in my heart with her gone, that no one else will ever be able to fill. And my heart hurts everyday for my youngest daughter who was only seven weeks old when "Dee" died. Sara will never know thee grandmother who loved to talk, sing and get down on the floor with her grandkids to play. She'll never taste the special meals Dee cooked, that I have never been able to duplicate. She'll never know the comfort of talking to Dee when you're feeling bad, and the special way that Dee had for making you feel better. She'll never know the total accepting love that Dee had so no matter what you may have done or said wrong. it didn't matter to her at all. I can only wish that somehow there is enough of "Dee" in my other two kids and myself, so somehow Sara can feel her through us. I pray that we'll all make the right choices in life so one day we'll join her again and Sara will know her grandmother's love first hand. Momma—I love you and miss you with all my heart.

Your daughter, Trish

It is time to remind ourselves that the "old" ways of doing things—traditional funerals followed by body burial, all taken care of by the funeral home—is not the only way of doing things.

We don't *have* to hold funeral services orchestrated by a funeral home. We don't *have* to commemorate the person who died in traditional ways. We *do* have to dispose of the body, but more and more people in North America are choosing cremation. And, as you well know, cremation can often be purchased without the help of a traditional funeral home.

At bottom, we as a culture—led by the Boomers—appear to be rethinking the importance of the funeral home and the funeral ritual. While funerals have been with us since the beginning of human history, many North Americans are now deciding that the funeral rituals of old are no longer meeting their needs and that the traditional funeral home isn't adding much value to the process.

Funeral service is at a crossroads. As a death educator and grief counselor, I am deeply concerned that individuals, families and ultimately society as a whole will suffer if those of you in funeral service do not take the lead in meeting the needs of the new customer.

If we step back and examine the true reasons for having funerals, we'll see that creating meaningful ceremonies when death impacts us can assist us with emotional, physical and spiritual transformations. The death of someone we love often temporarily disconnects us from ourselves and the world around us. As we search for some sense of balance, we must make internal adaptations to our new outer reality—someone who has been physically present in our lives is gone. Participating in a meaningful funeral ceremony helps us begin to recenter ourselves, to make that painful but necessary transition from life before the death to life after the death. In my work with thousands of bereaved people, however, I have found that many people—particularly Boomers—do not understand why funeral ceremonies help us adapt to change and help us heal (at least not until they have experienced a meaningful funeral service).

At bottom, we as a culture—led by the Boomers—appear to be rethinking the importance of the funeral home and the funeral ritual.

So, for many Boomers, traditional funeral rituals are devoid of value and meaning. They perceive them as empty and lacking creativity. I don't blame them. I myself have attended way too many of what I would term generic funerals—cookie cutter ceremonies that leave you feeling like you may as well have been at a stranger's funeral. As more and more people attend these meaningless funerals, society's opinion of the funeral ritual in general nosedives. This in turn causes people to devalue the funeral that will be held for them someday: "When I die, don't go to any trouble." A tendency to minimize one's own funeral is for many a reflection of the sense of purposelessness they have witnessed while attending generic funeral services.

But Boomers weren't born questioning the need for funerals. Products of the times in which they were born, they grew into this mindset. Here are a number of the influences that have shaped Boomer likes and dislikes, wants and needs, concerning funerals.

• *We live in the world's first death-free generation*

Many Boomers now live into their 40s and 50s before they experience a close personal loss. Today two-thirds of all deaths in the U.S. each year happen to people 65 or older. One result of this mortality rate shift is that if you are 40 or older and have never attended a truly meaningful funeral, you probably don't realize the importance of having one.

In the early 1900s, on the other hand, most children had been to many funerals by the age of ten. (In 1900 over half of all deaths in the U.S. were deaths of children 15 or younger.) Aging, illness and death were an everyday part of family life. While we certainly appreciate the medical advances that have helped lower the mortality rate and prolong lifespans, they are also distancing us from aging, illness, death, grief—and thus the funeral ritual.

• *We live in a mobile, fast-paced culture.*

Tremendous geographical distances often separate family members and friends today. Fifty years ago, friends only had to walk down the street to be a part of a funeral; now it is not unusual for them to fly in from thousands of miles away. This isn't convenient, and we are a convenience-based culture. If it isn't easy, we often just don't do it.

The Industrial Revolution brought about mass production and with it an emphasis on speed, efficiency and productivity. Then came the Techno-Revolution, heightening our ability to work faster, travel faster, communicate faster. We have come not just to want but to expect instant gratification—overnight delivery, cellular telephones, e-mail in a second, microwave popcorn, one-hour photo finishing, instant credit and home pregnancy tests. Other time-compressed, mind-shifting technologies include instant, worldwide news, video teleconferencing and hamburgers in less than 90 seconds.

> *We have come not just to want but to expect instant gratification—overnight delivery, cellular telephones, e-mail in a second, microwave popcorn, one-hour photo finishing, instant credit and home pregnancy tests.*

These examples of instant gratification change our frame of reference, our expectations, our values. Partly because we're busier and partly because we've come to expect it, we demand faster ways of doing things. And, unfortunately, we often confuse efficiency with effectiveness. When people get too busy, the first thing to go are rituals—from eating together to vacations to attending funerals. Yes, it may be easier not to spend time with the body. Yes, it may be easier to eliminate the visitation. Oh yes, it is easier not to play music that might make us sad. And the list of "easier" goes on and on and on . . .

Yet, easier isn't always better. To slow down and embrace elements of ceremony is effective, but not always efficient. After all, planning a personalized, meaningful funeral takes time, stirs up emotion, and doesn't really create any "closure." So, some say, "What's the use?" "Why go through all that?"

Many North Americans work hard, strive for efficiency, get things done, and, to draw on popular business and organizational terminology, measure outcomes. Many efficiency-minded people are uncomfortable having experiences they can't measure or control. Funeral experiences, by their very nature, encourage people to give up control, embrace pain, accept outside support, and feel instead of think.

Pragmatists tend to be overly focused on "bottom line" results and outcomes they can assess. But this tendency creates problems in the quest to "overcome" or "resolve" grief, because grief is not something you overcome, it is something you experience. In embracing one's grief, there is no "bottom line." Participating in an experience you can't "control" is a most impractical thing to do. Imagine crying openly and acknowledging the need for the support of family, friends and the greater community. That would simply not be the efficient thing to do! After all, meaningful funeral experiences help you encounter the sacred, and the sacred does not succumb to our instruments of assessment and measurement. As one efficient person I recently overhead said, "What's the point in having a funeral. It doesn't bring the dead person back to life!"

Of course, you don't have to be Alan Greenspan to understand that efficiency lowers costs and that lower costs are always better. So, some people reason that direct cremation (with no services) offers the best of both worlds; it's efficient AND cheap. As you know, it's also an emotionally hollow, non-experience that complicates the survivors' grief forever.

• *We're disconnected from each other.*

Many people have lost a sense of community. Not long ago, people shared their lives with those around them. Generation after generation, families lived in the same town or at least the same state. Neighbors visited on the front porch, gathered for meals and took care of each other's children. People knew each other. People watched out for each other. People cared about each other. Now, like no other time in history, many people feel alone and unconnected to groups.

One recent study found that 71 percent of Americans didn't know their neighbors. Adults and children alike live among strangers. The number of people who report they never spend time with their neighbors has doubled in only the last twenty years.

And just a few years ago Welcome Wagon closed up shop because no one's home to answer the door anymore. In 1968, this personal "welcome to our community" service logged 1.5 million face-to-face visits across the U.S. In 1997 that number had dropped to about half a million.

What's more, in the beginning of this century, only 10 percent of people lived in big cities. Now, more than 40 percent do. The irony is that when more people lived outside the city there was a greater sense of community.

We have evolved from a country of primary relationships to one of secondary relationships. Primary relationships are ones in which people know each other in a variety of roles—as friends, neighbors, co-workers. Secondary relationships are ones in which people are merely acquaintances. We may sit next to someone at work, but often we don't know much about him—where he lives, if he has a family, what his hobbies are.

As we have connected to the Internet, we have disconnected from each other.

As we have connected to the Internet, we have disconnected from each other. Names on the Net aren't always even real names. Our state-of-the-art technology has created a new kind of person, one who is plugged into machines instead of fellow human beings. Some of us talk more to voice mail than we do to our own family members.

• *We value self-reliance.*

Have you noticed that the biggest section in bookstores these days is the self-help section? We live in an era of rugged individualism and independence. We reward people for "doing it on their own." How many of us grew up learning the North American motto, "If you want it done right, do it yourself"? Yet, when someone in your life dies, you must be interdependent and connected to the world around you if you are to heal. In short, rugged individualism and funerals don't make good bedfellows.

For some, the goals of self-sufficiency and self-determination are the principle centerpieces of self-development. We are encouraged to think of ourselves as individual centers of consciousness, with the capacity for logical analysis. So, some logically (so they THINK) reason: "The person is dead, we don't need to see the body" and "We don't need to gather together, that won't change anything." As we use our individual "heads," we seem to be forgetting our "hearts," as well as our allegiance to the greater needs of the community. In sum, more and more people suffer from self-preoccupation, self-absorption, and self-fixation.

Funeral ceremonies are intended to activate support systems among one's family, friends and greater community. The trends towards privatization and elimination of funeral ceremonies, in part, reflect our placing of self interests over community interest.

To make matters worse, a favorite line of many pre-need marketers is, "Save your family the burden!" So, some people in funeral service play right into the hands of the person who has internalized the message: PUT SELF BEFORE COMMUNITY. As one person said to me recently, "Yes, I'll save my family the burden. When I die I'm just going to have them call 1-800-DIRECT DISPOSITION."

• *We eschew spiritualism.*

As our society becomes more educated, we seem to be adopting a more academic orientation to life and death. As I travel throughout North America, I observe that some of the largest pocket areas of direct cremation with no ceremony are in highly populated, academic communities. In a 1962 study, noted sociologist Robert Fulton confirmed that people who doubt the usefulness of funerals are more likely to be highly educated, professionally employed and financially well-off. Observational research of today is consistent with Fulton's 30-year-old findings.

Of course, many among this highly educated population would argue they have found a substitute for the old-fashioned, "morbid" funeral: the memorial service. It seems that the more educated one becomes, the more "at risk" one becomes for not participating in death rituals. The potential problem with memorial services is twofold: 1) they are often delayed until a more convenient time weeks or months after the death, and 2) the body is often not present. These factors tend to encourage mourners to skirt the healing pain that funerals—because of their timeliness, their focus on embracing a variety of feelings, including pain (not just joy), and their use of the body as reality check—set in motion. How many times have you heard someone leave a memorial service saying, "Wasn't that great! No one even cried!" While some memorials are certainly meaningful and authentic, I am suggesting that too often they do healthy mourning a disservice.

• *We don't understand the role of pain and suffering.*

Another major influence on the deritualization of death in our culture is our avoidance of pain. We misunderstand the role of suffering. People who openly express their feelings of grief are often told to "carry on," "keep your chin up" or "just keep busy." Worse yet, some bereaved people are greeted with theologized clichés like "God wouldn't give you any more than you can bear," and "Look at it this way . . . now you have an angel in heaven." This misuse of doctrine is used by some for the purpose of suppressing "incorrect" thoughts and feelings. Shame-based messages like the above examples result in some bereaved people thinking that mourning (i.e. sharing your grief outside yourself) is bad. If you are perceived as "doing well" with your grief, on the other hand, you are considered "strong" and "under control." Of course, it is easier to stay "rational" if you don't participate in a ceremony that is intended to, among other things, encourage you to embrace feelings and acknowledge a painful reality.

We misunderstand the role of suffering.

• *We have lost the symbolism of death.*

Deritualization also appears to be influenced by a loss of death's symbols. Ariès, in his book *The Hour of Our Death*, identifies the symbols representing death in art and in literature, as well as in funeral and burial customs. He maintains, and I agree, that symbols of death are no longer prominent in contemporary North American culture, and that gone with them is a link that in previous generations provided meaning and a sense of continuity for the living.

In generations past, for example, the bereaved used to wear mourning clothes or armbands, often black, that symbolized their sorrow. In some subcultures, mourners also hung wreaths on the door to let others know that someone loved had died. Today we can't even tell who the bereaved are. For some, memorial flowers, both at the funeral and at the cemetery, are becoming another ousted symbol. Today we opt for the more practical but less spiritual monetary donation: "In lieu of flowers, please send contributions to . . ."

Perhaps the ultimate symbol of death that we are tending more and more to forsake is the dead person's body. When viewed at the visitation or during the funeral service itself, the body encourages mourners to confront the reality and the finality of the death. Of course, opponents of viewing often describe it as unseemly, expensive, undignified and unnecessary. Yet, seeing and spending time with the body allows for last goodbyes and visual confirmation that someone loved is indeed dead. In generations past, the body often served as the very locus of mourning; the bereaved came to the dead person's home to view the body, pay their last respects and support the primary mourners. In fact, the body was often displayed for days before burial. Today, with our increasing reliance on closed caskets and cremation before or with no ceremony, we are forgetting the importance of this tradition.

As Ariès writes, "The change (in death's role in our society) consists precisely in banishing from the sight of the public not only death but with it, its icon. Relegated to the secret, private space of the home or the anonymity of the hospital, death no longer makes any sign." As we eliminate the symbols of death, we also appear to be eliminating the rituals, historically rich in symbolism, that remind us of the death of others as well as our own ultimate demise.

• *We deny our own mortality.*

One woman said to me recently, "I don't do death." She is not alone. Many people in North America today deny their own mortality and thus the need for rituals surrounding death. In his book *The Funeral: Vestige or Value,* author Paul Irion calls this "assumed invulnerability."

He reflects that, "Man knows that he is only assuming invulnerability, that he is ultimately vulnerable, and yet to admit this fact totally is to be defenseless." In other words, denying our own mortality is better than the alternative.

The single most important thing to know about Americans . . . is that they think death is optional.

Sigmund Freud also wrote of this theme when he concluded, "At bottom no one believes in his own death, or to put the same thing in another way, in the unconscious every one of us is convinced of his own immortality."

Author Jane Walmsley summed up well the current North American mindset about death when she wrote, "The single most important thing to know about Americans . . . is that they think death is optional." Unfortunately, today we do believe that mourning, if it is to be done at all, should be done quickly and privately—three days off work then back to the normal routine. No time for planning ceremonies. No need to drag out the pain. No use in dwelling on death. Should these messages continue to be internalized, we will see the continued deritualization of death in our culture.

• *We devalue life.*

Sad to say, but many children and adults have become desensitized to the meaning and value of life as well as death. I recently read about a new fad on school playgrounds. Children are bringing laser pens to school and using them for pretend "lasergunfights" at recess. The tragic and all-too-real school shootings of late only compound the irony of this violent play.

Television has presented a distorted image of the significance of a human life. Simply by turning on the TV, we are exposed to a multitude of examples of violent death each day. All too often, themes of violence take center stage in our books, movies, video and computer games, and music, too. Internalizing these powerful images can result in a cynical view of life in general, let alone the need to have ceremonies when someone loved dies.

Many of today's kids are not being taught to value life. How are they ever to learn to value and respect death?

• *We value . . . what do we value?*

Many North Americans appear to be facing an enemy from within —a crisis of meaning and values.

The media teaches us to value consumerism, as if we can somehow buy our happiness. Many children would rather watch TV than go for a walk in the woods. Some children and adults have been coerced by the media into believing they should meet every want, buy every product, and do it now. As the Nike commercial says, "Just Do It!"

Many families have become disconnected from each other and the natural world. Did you know that 4 in 10 children today don't live with their biological fathers and that 40% of these children haven't even seen their fathers for at least a year? Values that were once taught by family, church and community are now, more often that not, taught through advertisements and mindless TV sitcoms. Our former president (who said, by the way, "Governments don't raise children, parents do") had to go before the grand jury and discuss his sex life and defend himself against perjury.

Our culture of immediate gratification, self-absorption, and deceit has confused us about what is right and wrong and good and bad. Many people don't have road maps for what family life should be like, let alone what a meaningful funeral should be like.

And we wonder why Boomers are questioning the need for funerals. . .

So What's a Funeral Home to Do?

For funeral service, the rise of the Boomers means that their customers will be more difficult to satisfy than in the past. Some observers have noted that the new customer is the "never satisfied customer."

Today's enlightened funeral home understands that the "never satisfied customer" is won only one way: through dynamic service.

Dynamically serving the customer means providing information, education and choices that meet individual needs and circumstances, creating authentic, meaningful funeral Experiences for each family served, and constantly working to make small, gradual improvements in the service you provide.

If we are honest with ourselves, we must admit that many in funeral service have internalized this assumption: "We know what our customers want and need even better than they do." Indeed, it is tempting to believe that years of experience "in the business" have made us omniscient. Can this kind of thinking get a funeral home in trouble quickly today? Not only can it, it already has for some.

Funeral homes that best understand that there is a new and very different customer out there will work to create and communicate a well-defined, customer-inspired service strategy. The funeral home of the future will be focused on listening to and understanding and responding swiftly and flexibly to the changing wants, needs and expectations of families served. The funeral home of the future will understand that families will expect and demand customization and personalization of every funeral. The funeral home of the future will create and maintain "customer-friendly" service delivery systems. The funeral home of the future will hire, inspire and develop customer-oriented staff. Funeral directors of the future will be facilitators, not functionaries.

Dynamically serving the customer means providing information, education and choices that meet individual needs and circumstances, creating authentic, meaningful funeral Experiences for each family served, and constantly working to make small, gradual improvements in the service you provide.

Even those of you who think your customer orientation is excellent shouldn't relax into smug self-congratulation. Boomer families are: more apt to use technology to consider choices (people are accessing wholesale casket prices on the Internet and bringing them into funeral homes with a demand to meet or beat the price); more diverse and mobile; and much more demanding of respectful and courteous treatment.

I challenge you to create a customer service strategy for your funeral home that addresses the trend to devalue the funeral. Examine how you have helped families in the past. Examine your strengths as well as your weaknesses. Look through your files and evaluate every funeral you've planned over the past year or two. Contact families and ask them what you could have done better. Ask yourselves what you could have done better. Be brutally honest. Encourage your staff to be brutally honest. The next time a new family walks through your door, break free of the old way of doing business and ask yourself how you can best meet the needs of this unique bereaved family.

The future of funeral service hinges on listening to the customer like never before. This means not only listening to the needs of each individual family—because the "new customer" is not in reality a demographic of millions but a single, unique family that has just experienced a single, unique death—but also paying close attention to trends and new requests.

If you lay them all out on the table and look for patterns, all the Boomer trends and requests point collectively to the topic of the next chapter, creating exceptional funeral Experiences for today's families. Boomers want good Experiences. Dynamic customer service results in good Experiences. So let's talk about this notion of Experiences and how you go about creating them for families.

A complete report on this study is available from Batesville.

Chapter 3

It's the **Experience** that Counts

I want you to close your eyes and think about the most meaningful days of your life.

Mull these thoughts over for a moment then settle on one certain experience for purposes of this exercise. Perhaps it is your wedding day or the birth of your child. Maybe it is a holiday memory, a special vacation time or a certain afternoon in the company of someone significant to you. Perhaps it is a day spent at the bedside of a loved one who was dying.

Do you have a particular experience in mind? Good. Now slowly walk through this memory. What made it so special? Who were you with? Why were you there? What were the surroundings like? What touch sensations do you recall? What sounds can you remember? What smells laced the air? Are there certain tastes you associate with this experience? I'll bet that if you concentrate hard enough and linger long enough in this room of your mind, you'll recall a symphony of sights, sounds, smells, tastes. You'll remember the thoughts and feelings you had. You may also consider, with the benefit of hindsight, how this experience changed your life.

The gift of memory is that such experiences live on in us forever. Whether joyful or sad, playful or emotionally weighty, memorable experiences form the very fabric of our lives, the warp and weft of who we are.

Sometimes the most memorable experiences of our lives occur spontaneously. Say you are eight years old and in mid-air, jumping off your backyard swing as you have done hundreds of times before. But this time you land akimbo and unbearable pain shoots up your leg. Your discerning mother takes you, sobbing, to the emergency room, where an xray reveals you have indeed broken your femur. Suddenly and without warning, an everyday experience has become a memorable one.

But perhaps more often, memorable experiences are the product of out-of-the-ordinary, scripted events. Weddings, birthdays, holidays, and vacations often form the backdrop for our most significant memories. Such events are ritualized. They have certain predictable and recognizable patterns and elements that guide us in carrying them out. American birthday parties, for example, require invitations, games and socializing, wrapped presents and a cake alight with candles, which are heartily blown out after a rousing chorus of "Happy Birthday to You."

Which brings me closer to my point. The funeral for someone you love is an out-of-the-ordinary, planned event. It is also a ritualized event, with certain predictable and recognizable patterns and elements. And since the death of someone loved is truly a life-changing experience, the funeral is, by default, a memorable experience.

Think about a funeral that touched you. Why did it touch you? Why was it more memorable than others? Who had died and why? Who was in attendance? What were the surroundings like? What touch sensations do you recall? What sounds can you remember? What smells laced the air? What were your thoughts and feelings at the time?

You have the power to shape people's lives, to orchestrate an exceptional, memorable experience that will help mourners heal and grow.

Here's the heart of the matter. If you agree that memorable experiences shape our lives and that the funeral can be one of life's most memorable experiences, then the funeral home plays an incredibly important role in the community and you as funeral director are pretty damned important. You have the power to shape people's lives, to orchestrate an exceptional, memorable experience that will help mourners heal and grow.

And that, my friends, is the key to your future success, both in terms of satisfying, meaningful work and profitability.

The Experience Economy
(with thanks to Gilmore and Pine)

I've long been a proponent of meaningful funeral ceremonies. In fact, in 1994 I wrote a book called *Creating Meaningful Funeral Ceremonies: A Guide for Caregivers*, which bemoaned the new customer's lack of understanding of the funeral's value and emphasized the importance of creating new, more personalized ceremonies that better meet Boomer needs.

I've spoken on this topic to hundreds of funeral directors, clergy and other bereavement caregivers across North America countless times in the last ten years. I told them, as I tell you now, that their businesses would not survive unless they changed the way they do things.

But until the 1999 NFDA Convention in Kansas City, when I sat in the audience and listened to keynote speaker and author James Gilmore say, "The Service Economy is peaking. A new, emerging economy is coming to the fore, one based on a distinct kind of economic output (experiences). Goods and services are no longer enough," I hadn't made the connection that what I was championing on behalf of funeral service was the creation of meaningful *experiences*. And, moreover, that it wasn't just funeral service that needed to make this shift but the *entire economy*.

Of course.

In his speech Gilmore explained how our economy has evolved from being commodities-based to goods-based to service-based, and now, to experience-based. This evolution of economic offerings can itself be instantiated in something as commonplace as the birthday cake.

Gilmore noted that in the agrarian economy, mothers made birthday cakes from scratch, mixing farm commodities (flour, sugar, butter, eggs) that together cost mere pennies. As the goods-based industrial economy advanced, moms paid a dollar or two to Betty Crocker for pre-mixed ingredients. Later, when the service economy took hold, busy parents ordered cakes from the bakery or grocery store, which, at $10 or $15, cost ten times more than the packaged ingredients. Now, in today's time-starved economy, parents neither make the birthday cake nor throw the party. Instead, they spend $100 or more to "outsource" the entire event to Chuck E. Cheese's, the Discovery Zone or some other business that stages memorable events for kids—and often throws in the cake for free.

And it turns out that the things that really matter— the things that give life meaning—aren't things at all but experiences.

Experiences, says Gilmore, are a fourth level of value (above commodities, goods and services) and thus can command a much higher price than mere goods or even excellent service. Boomers want and are willing to pay for memorable experiences. They may buy the less expensive toothpaste or contract with the cheapest lawn care service in town, but they are more than willing to pony up for lattés at

Starbucks, vacations at Club Med, and the "Total Ownership Experience" of Lexus. Unyoked of the abbreviated lifespans and hardships of generations past, and beneficiaries of the strongest economy in the history of the world, they're more affluent, more educated and more able to turn their attention to "the things that really matter."

And it turns out that the things that really matter—the things that give life meaning—aren't things at all but *experiences*.

In the last chapter we explored common Boomer wants and complaints about funeral service. They typically want more information and more ideas for personalization. They increasingly want cremation. They often don't care about the casket. Some days it feels like they're picking on just funeral service, but they're not. They're voicing similar wants and complaints about restaurants, clothing, education, home design, etc. etc. etc.. Across the board, Boomers want engaging experiences. Funeral service just happens to be an old-fashioned, traditional goods- and services-based industry that might suffer more growing pains because it may have to be dragged, kicking and screaming, into the Experience Economy.

So I returned home from the NFDA Convention buzzing with new ideas and connections. And I read Gilmore's book, *The Experience Economy: Work is Theatre & Every Business a Stage* (Harvard Business School Press, 1999), which he coauthored with his business partner, B. Joseph Pine II. I found that the concept of creating meaningful funeral experiences could be further explored in context of the Experience Economy. The remainder of this chapter does this.

Before we go much further, however, I should point out to you that experiences are not synonymous with entertainment. Don't dismiss the experience concept because it conjures up images of funeral directors tap-dancing in tails alongside the casket. While the visionary Walt Disney and others who followed in his footsteps certainly foresaw and capitalized on the value of entertaining experiences, companies stage an experience whenever they engage customers in a personal, memorable way. Experiences engage, preferably on emotional, physical, intellectual and even spiritual levels; they don't necessarily entertain. And buying those experiences is akin to buying a series of memories. If that doesn't describe funeral service at its best, I don't know what does.

The Realms of Experience

If experiences aren't about entertaining but engaging, what constitutes a non-entertaining experience? There are four "realms of experience," according to

Pine and Gilmore, and entertainment is just one. You can guess what the entertainment realm is all about (think Disney again). The other three are *educational, escapist and esthetic.*

In the educational realm, customers learn as part of their experience. Here at the Center for Loss in Fort Collins, Colorado, I teach a number of week-long courses to bereavement caregivers each year. Groups of 18 caregivers, such as hospice workers, funeral directors, physicians, and clergy, gather to learn from me and each other. Their experience includes five days of interactive, discussion-based content, as well as sharing their own personal stories of loss, listening to music, enjoying meals together and hiking in the rugged mountain foothills around the Center. The Center itself is a lovely hexagonal-shaped building with many windows, comfortable seating and a tasteful decor. Consciously, I have set the stage to make this week of education as much of an experience as possible for everyone who participates.

The escapist realm, on the other hand, immerses customers in a totally different reality. Examples of escapist environments include theme parks, chat rooms, laser tag centers and casinos. Have you ever tried to find your way around a mirrored, labyrinthine casino without getting lost or disoriented? Casino designers are very good at creating escapist experiences. Escapist experiences actively involve customers; people come to "do" in the escapist realm.

In the esthetic realm, people come just to "be." This realm immerses people in unique and often awesome events or environments in a passive way. Relaxing on the ocean shore, viewing the Louvre's Mona Lisa, gazing up at a lunar eclipse, soaking up the atmosphere in Time's Square—these are esthetic experiences.

The Four Realms of Experience

Entertainment

Using ideas such as tasteful humor in a eulogy and talented live musicians, and, especially, designing a beautiful, comfortable gathering room that encourages family and friends to linger and enjoy each other's company.

Educational

Giving the consumer the opportunity to learn about funerals and why they are important. This can be accomplished by leaving out pamphlets or giving talks to community groups.

Escapist

Encouraging families to actively engage in activities during the visitation, funeral and committal. These can range from lighting candles to standing up and sharing memories to laying flowers on the casket.

Esthetic

Creating a positive atmosphere, one that engages all the senses and in which people feel good about spending their time. This can involve good lighting, quality sound systems and other subtle but extremely important cues.

Funerals traditionally are esthetic experiences. People come to funerals just to "be there," to demonstrate their support and love by their presence. For the most part, they do not play an active role in the funeral itself, but rather "take in" the sights, the sounds, the readings, the music. They allow their thoughts and feelings to wash over them as they focus on the life and death of the person who died.

Esthetic funeral experiences are wonderful and healing, particularly when funeral homes do a good job of creating a sense of place, engaging all the senses and eliminating negative cues—topics discussed later in this chapter. However, exceptional funeral planning attempts to integrate more than one realm of experience for bereaved families and friends. The escapist realm, in particular, offers many possibilities for funeral directors; indeed, we are already seeing a trend toward escapist funerals.

The escapist realm would ask: What can bereaved families and friends "do" at the visitation or funeral to further immerse themselves in the experience? When you sit down with families and actively engage them in arranging the funeral (see Arranging), you are creating an escapist experience. When family members and friends participate in the service by giving readings, playing music, sharing memories and lighting candles, they are in escapist realm territory. When funeral guests not only sign the guestbook but are asked to write down a specific memory of the person who died, they are venturing into the escapist realm. When people lay flowers or throw dirt atop the casket at the close of the committal service, they are in the escapist realm of experience. Anything you as a funeral director can do to present families with "escapist" options—never forcing them but encouraging them to take advantage of these healing activities—helps create an exceptional funeral Experience.

The escapist realm would ask: What can bereaved families and friends "do" at the visitation or funeral to further immerse themselves in the experience?

The educational realm is also not out of place in funeral service. A few years back I launched a program called "Honoring Family Choices" in conjunction with Batesville Management Services. Honoring Family Choices is a series of signage and literature for display in funeral homes that teaches the importance of funerals and the elements of ceremony. The signs ask, for example, "Why do we have funerals?" then provides answers in simple, direct language. Your funeral home brochure and website (see W for Website) should also educate consumers and community members about what you do and why. Giving talks to service clubs and other community organizations about the history and importance of funeral service is yet another way to capitalize on the educational realm.

The entertainment realm of experience can also be used to great effect in funeral planning. While few would term the funeral an "entertaining" experience, humor is certainly an appropriate part of many eulogies. The gathering or reception after the funeral is perhaps the best time to consider the entertainment realm: tasty and visually-appetizing foods; memory tables filled with memorabilia that encourages mourners to reminisce about "the good times;" more festive decorating and lighting; round tables surrounded by upholstered chairs. All these things encourage family and friends to stay, to stick around, to talk and enjoy each other's company. Funeral homes would be well-served to consider the entertainment realm as they plan the building or remodeling of their reception spaces.

According to Gilmore and Pine, "When all four realms abide within a single setting, then and only then does plain space become a distinctive place for staging an experience. Occuring over a period of time, staged experiences require a sense of place to entice guests to spend more time engaged in the offering."

Are you creating staged experiences with a sense of place worthy of a family's time, money and love for the person who died?

A Sense of Place

Funeral homes establish a sense of place largely through their facility design. What does your funeral home look like, inside and out? What message does the decor and the layout send to bereaved families? Is it inviting, clean, well kept, not worn, easy to move around?

Many companies in the Experience Economy are "theming" their offerings; think of the Rainforest Café, Niketown, and the San Diego Zoo's Wild Animal Park. I bid you to consider the "theme" of your funeral home. Is it dark, formal and heavily patterned in its wallpaper and upholstery? Is it nondescript? Is it angular, *A funeral home with the person who has died as theme will be the perfect fit for every family who walks through your door.* clean-lined and contemporary? No single environment will suit all bereaved families. But a funeral home with the person who has died as theme will be the perfect fit for every family who walks through your door.

The person who died as theme? Think of your funeral home as a blank slate. It's your job to customize the space as much as possible for every new family.

Certainly you'll have to choose or work within an existing architectural style. But if you make the spaces beautifully lit, simply decorated—perhaps with plants, wooden furniture, and neutral fabrics—and comfortable, you can then "set the stage" for each unique funeral or visitation.

Did the person who died love lilacs? Fill the visitation room with lilacs. Did the person who died make quilts? Hang her quilts on all the walls and atop the casket. Did the person who died play the bass? Create a display of his beautiful instrument and sheet music, together with photos of him playing the bass. Was the person who died first and foremost a mother? Place the tools of her trade around the room: books she read to her children; toys she lovingly tended for them; photos of her and her children together. I know a funeral home that set the stage for a horse lover who died by placing his casket on top of hay bales and "saddling up" the casket.

At Flanner & Buchanan Mortuaries in Indiana, each family that calls is asked to bring a photograph of the person who died to the arrangement conference. The funeral home has a local media company enlarge the photo to portrait size and places it in a beautiful frame with the name and dates of the person who died. The portrait is set on an easel by the register book and is presented to the family after services. A little touch, yes, but one that has made a much better Experience for Flanner & Buchanan customers.

Of course, the funeral home isn't the only place to hold visitations or funerals. In addition to churches or other places of worship, funerals can be held almost anywhere: barns, meadows, golf courses, riverbanks. If the person who died is the theme, where would be the most meaningful place to hold the ceremony? Somewhere meaningful to the person who died or to her family. (See L for Location.)

Now's also a good time to emphasize the importance and versatility of photos in creating a sense of place and, ultimately, an exceptional funeral experience. Many funeral homes encourage families to create memory boards or bring in a framed photo or two to display. But if you're truly setting the stage, it's your job as funeral director to creatively and effectively display photos. Yes, I agree that it's healing for family members themselves to gather and organize photos for a memory board or display. There's so much more that can be done with those same photos! Beacham McDougald Funeral Home and Crematorium in North Carolina routinely creates "Life Reflections" photo shows that are displayed on a 36" color TV at the visitation. (See Visitation for details.) You can also buy large format printers that will print oversized images of photos you've scanned in. Imagine several poster-size photos of the person who died, placed in simple poster frames and hung on the visitation room or chapel walls instead of blah prints or paintings. Do you have display easels or stands for photo albums? Do you have the means to edit home videos and play them at the funeral? Do you use scanned photos of the person who died in personalized programs? Does your website post obituaries and online "guestbooks"?

Personalizing your space in honor of the person who died helps create an experience that's about the person who died and the people who loved him—not about your decorator's taste or your funeral home's history (how many funeral homes prominently display photos from their company's past but don't offer to do the same for the family of the person who died?). It further immerses families in the esthetic and escapist realms. It encourages them to stay, to spend time together, in contemplation and honor of the unique person who died.

> *Personalizing your space in honor of the person who died helps create an experience that's about the person who died and the people who loved him—not about your decorator's taste or your funeral home's history.*

As those of you who already focus on creating a sense of place know, personalization of this sort takes some extra time and energy. Creative photo use also takes a working understanding of technologies such as computers, scanners, printers, DVDs, etc. Your pricing structure should compensate you for these value-added, experience-oriented services. After all, these are just the sort of things Boomers and X- and Y-geners value and are more than willing to pay for.

Positive and Negative Cues

One of your main responsibilities in creating exceptional funeral experiences is ensuring that every impression families have of your funeral home is a good one. Every impression. Every single one.

When passersby drive past your funeral home, what impression do they get? When a family first phones you, what impression do they get? (See Telephones.) When they see your Yellow Pages ad, what impression do they get? When you go to their home to remove the body, what impression do they get? When they walk in your front door, what impression do they get? When they sit down with you to arrange the funeral, what impression do they get? When they view the body for the first time, what impression do they get?

Each of these key steps in the funeral planning chain of events is a Moment of Truth and merits scrutiny. Individually they form a largely unconscious (but nonetheless indelible) impression in your customer's mind. They are the main moments in time in which a customer judges who you are. Collectively these moments form the backbone of the Experience the customer will have with your funeral home.

In addition to Moments of Truth, other, seemingly more minor impressions contribute to the Experience. Take your funeral home's layout, for example. Is it easy for families to find their way to the right visitation room or the chapel or the restroom—or do people tend to get lost or disoriented? (The latter makes good business sense for casinos but definitely not for funeral homes.) Or consider the jargon you might sometimes use in front of families. (See Words.) Have you ever said, "Where is the deceased now?" instead of the preferable "Where is your mother/Edna now?" Also think about how your funeral home smells, how the upholstery feels, how the background music or other noises contribute to the experience.

Emphasize positive cues and eliminate negative cues if you truly want to improve your level of service and create exceptional funeral experiences for today's families.

Emphasize positive cues and eliminate negative cues if you truly want to improve your level of service and create exceptional funeral experiences for today's families. Bring in an objective outsider—not a funeral service "expert"—and create a mock funeral planning experience for her. Afterwards, ask her how she felt during the various Moments of Truth and which cues she found negative, which positive. Or better yet, have an objective outsider interview several families you've served recently. Take this feedback seriously and make changes where necessary.

Engage the Five Senses

We've already discussed the sense of place your facility creates and the positive and negative cues families get when they come in contact with your funeral home. Part of enhancing positive cues and thus the funeral experience for today's families involves engaging all five senses.

At the beginning of this chapter I asked you to think about a particularly memorable experience. Chances are you can remember many sensory details, including sights, sounds, tastes, textures, and smells. In fact, the more an experience engages all five senses, the more memorable it is.

For funeral service, you might consider the impact of the following sensory input on the overall Experience:

Sense	Cues
Sight	Facility decor, lighting, colors, the body, memorabilia displays and other elements of personalization, cleanliness
Sound	Music, readings, squeaky doors or floorboards, sound system quality, acoustics, background noises (heating, air conditioning, nearby traffic, etc.)
Touch	Upholstery, seating comfort, the body, the casket, touchable memorabilia displays, the program
Smell	Flowers, embalming/chemical smells, food
Taste	At reception: food quality, selection, tastiness; mints, drinks or other refreshments you offer guests during the arrangement conference or visitation

How can you improve or enhance the ways in which you engage families' senses? One relatively inexpensive and simple way that comes to mind is lighting. I think a funeral home's lighting should be warm and bright but not harsh. Well-placed cans or hanging fixtures can create an inviting mood for display tables and conversation areas. Consider adding windows to dark rooms or revamping window treatments to allow for better lighting. How is the lighting in your facility? What mood does it create? Bring in a talented lighting designer and see what he thinks.

How is the lighting in your facility? What mood does it create?

Sound system quality is another important sensory cue. Have you ever listened to music on really good, really well placed speakers? It's like the difference between flying first class and flying in the cargo hold. Music helps mourners embrace their feelings. It immerses them in the experience. Poor sound quality, feedback and other audio problems jolt them out of the experience. Investing in good sound equipment (and video equipment, too) is definitely one of the most important investments you can make.

It's easy to overlook the sense of smell in funeral planning. The field of aromatherapy has many ideas to offer. Scented candles might be just right for some visitations or funerals (think vanilla for someone who liked to bake or pine for an outdoorsperson). Aroma oils in scents of lavender or citrus or mint could add a nice touch. Flowers with distinctive smells are always appropriate. Like too much perfume, too much scent or too many competing scents are bad ideas. But used sparingly and chosen with care based on the likes and dislikes of the person who died and her family, scent can make an experience come alive and awaken poignant memories.

I'm sure you can think of many more ways to engage all five senses of the families you serve if you think creatively and with an open mind. Whatever you do, don't discount this subtle but critical facet of creating exceptional funeral experiences.

Charging for Experiences

Funeral service is falling prey to commoditization. Many funeral homes and "alternative" funeral service providers are competing based on low prices: "We can do it all for $595," "Lowest prices in town." So, at the same time Gilmore observes that people are seeking experiences (and believes, as do many of us, that this applies to funeral service), much of the advertising we now witness in funeral service is based on competing on the basis of price for goods (commodities).

What if you created a pricing structure that built little if any profits into the casket and other products you sell and instead firmly planted your profits where they belong—in the valuable, value-added Experiences you help families create?

Let's learn from Gilmore's very words: "While customers love a sale, businesses perish from relying on low prices . . . that system of competition no longer sustains growth and profitability. You know it; we all know it. But what do we do about it?"

What we do about it is create exceptional funeral experiences, which we know Boomers value and are willing to pay for, then charge accordingly for those experiences. Gone are the days when the sale of the casket and other products could support your funeral home. Going are the days when simply charging a "service fee" for the basic services you render is justifiable to customers. They want more bang for their buck, more Experience and less focus on goods and services.

Gilmore and Pine give the example of computer giant IBM. At first IBM offered free service to support computer sales until the computer industry matured to the point that the computer itself was of less value than the service behind it. So then IBM started buying its industrial customers' mainframe computers for them if they would contract with IBM's Global Services to manage their IS business. Flip-flop.

What if you created a pricing structure that built little if any profits into the casket and other products you sell and instead firmly planted your profits where they belong—in the valuable, value-added Experiences you help families create? Can you imagine the feeling of empowerment (and creativity-inducing, constructive pressure) this would place on you and your staff to indeed create exceptional funeral Experiences for families? After all, if you're charging for incredible funerals, you will have no choice but to deliver on that promise.

And what if, as Pine and Gilmore suggest, you conceived of charging admission to your funerals? Now I realize you can't and won't literally charge admission. But the key question here is: What would you do differently if you were charging admission? Your answers to this question will help you make the shift from commodities and services to the Experience Economy.

I agree with Pine and Gilmore that the Experience Economy is a fourth and higher level of economic offerings. Boomers and X- and Y-geners value experiences are willing to pay for them. You are in a position to provide those experiences, to differentiate yourself among area funeral homes. For many families, it won't matter if you charge more to plan and carry out the funeral IF you create the best experiences. *What would you do differently if you were charging admission?* Families and community members will come away from your funerals saying, "Wow. That was absolutely the best funeral I ever attended. I never knew a funeral could be so powerful, so meaningful, so healing." Word of mouth will spread and calls to your funeral home will grow. So will your bottom line, if you're charging accordingly for the value you provide. It's a win-win situation for families and for funeral service.

Before moving on to the A-Z section of this book, let's pause for a second and remind ourselves of what we've covered so far. We've looked at some of the key reasons for what I've called the funeral service "customer service crisis." We've met the Boomers and reviewed what it is they want and why. And we've been introduced to the concept of creating memorable funeral Experiences for today's families. We've built the framework; now it's time to to dig into the nuts and bolts of customer service excellence.

"We were into things, but now we're into experiences."

Part Two

A-Z: An Alphabetical Exploration of Key Customer Service Issues in Funeral Service

The title of this book promises to cover funeral home customer service issues from A-Z. Well, here they come, all 75 of them. I invite you to flip through the remainder of this book and read those sections that seem most pertinent to your funeral home right now. Then, and here's the really important part, begin creating a plan to turn your funeral home into an Experience-maker (or improve your Experience-staging strengths if you're already on your way).

How do you make such a plan? As you read, jot down notes in the margins. Insert your specific funeral home into every topic and example in this book and, judging critically, measure yourself. How does your funeral home rate? What are your strengths and weaknesses? Write them down, along with ideas for changing or improving (even your strengths demand scrutiny and continual improvement).

Then get together with your staff (ask them to read this book first) and have everyone together brainstorm customer service enhancements. To help you focus, maybe you could have individual meetings on some of the A-Z topics that are most critical for your funeral home right now. For example, hold a meeting on First Impressions and together with your staff, create an action plan with measurable goals and completion dates to better your delivery in this critical area.

It's best to write a comprehensive long-term plan in pursuit of customer service excellence, broken up into shorter-term, discrete and measurable goals. But if that seems overwhelming, just get started on one topic that you're motivated to work on, then move on to the next. Little improvements here and there ultimately add up to big ones.

I wish you luck. I wish you good health. I wish you tenacity. But most of all I wish you the vision to truly see the amazing possibilities for your funeral home, because once you've peeked over that horizon, there'll be no stopping you. And you and the families you are privileged to serve will be changed forever in memorable, transforming ways.

Aftercare

Aftercare is a relatively new offering in funeral service, dating back to the early '70s with the formation of widow and widower programs. Contemporary aftercare in funeral homes ranges from making grief literature available to providing individual counseling.

In a landmark text in this area of service, funeral home aftercare was defined as:

> An organized way to maintain a helpful and caring relationship with clients, offer continuing services to client families beyond the expected body disposition and accompanying rituals, and provide death, loss and grief education to both clients and the community (Weeks and Johnson, 2001).

Aftercare services appear to vary widely depending on the philosophy of the funeral home, the resources available and the needs of the community. As aftercare gained popularity in the '80s and '90s, a number of funeral homes began to offer some form of follow-up with families served. Elements of aftercare might include telephone calls, personal visits, cards, grief support groups, educational workshops, holiday services, bereavement camp for children, etc. A number of funeral homes also provide educational resources, such as lending libraries, newsletters, and referral resources to trained professionals.

In their timely and helpful resource *When All The Funerals Have Gone* (Baywood Publishing, ISBN 0-89503-215-5, hardcover, 264 pp.), my colleagues Duane Weeks and Catherine Johnson have assembled an interesting and insightful variety of articles on establishing bereavement aftercare programs. Section 1 of the book examines the emergence and formalizing of funeral home aftercare programs. Section 2 explores aftercare provided at schools, community grief centers, hospitals and military settings. Lastly, Section 3 focuses on general issues of interest to those administering or providing clinical services in bereavement aftercare. An index provides a helpful way to access the significant information contained in this comprehensive resource. Add this book to your library today!

In their book, Weeks and Johnson have identified and conceptualized four categories of aftercare programs:

The CASUAL classification includes visiting with mourners, meeting a grieving person on the street or by chance, and sharing book lists and brochures.

The FUNDAMENTAL category includes making telephone calls, sending newsletters, and hosting social dinners or travel.

The STANDARD level includes facilitating support groups, lending library materials, and sponsoring special holiday programs or community education and sending cards on special days.

The PREMIERE category includes individual counseling, children's programs, in-service training, community advisory boards, and acting as a spokesperson for the media.

Obviously, each of these categories requires different levels of staffing and commitment of resources. Whatever category or combination of categories you decide on, compassionate aftercare is a critical part of today's families' Experience with your funeral home. From informal aftercare provided by sincere, caring staff members to retaining a licensed counselor on staff, your funeral home has an opportunity to support families after the death.

Several considerations should be an important part of the planning, implementation, or refining of your aftercare program. These considerations would include but should not be limited to the following:

- Needs assessment
- Program design (different levels of aftercare you might provide)
- Personnel selection
- Training of personnel
- Selection of educational resource material
- Program evaluation

A special note: Remember, it is unprofessional and unethical to combine aftercare visits with any kind of sales presentation. If a family member requests information about prepaid funerals or other services not yet provided, they should be referred to appropriate staff members.

So again, what is aftercare? I asked my friend Paul Pyrch, Aftercare Coordinator for H.D. Oliver in Virginia, what he thinks aftercare should consist of. He writes:

A well-conceived aftercare program provides people with vital information on grief and mourning, the best educational materials available and the tools they need to handle their own grief work in ways appropriate to them. It offers nonjudgemental support and an atmosphere of trust in which bereaved families may receive assistance not only to cope with their losses, but also to grow through them and to understand the healing value of their grief and mourning.

Without some level of aftercare, your funeral home is missing out on a tremendous opportunity to advocate for the needs of the families you are privileged to serve. First impressions are critical, but so are last impressions, which are the purpose of aftercare. You can create a truly exceptional Experience for the family, but unless you follow through you haven't made the Experience all it can or should be. You also haven't lived up to your promises to the family, and the family may well develop a relationship with a different funeral home that does provide ongoing contact and support.

Arranging

The arrangement conference is where the Experience plan is created. It sets the tone for all that will follow.

During the typical arrangement conference, the funeral director generally uses a preprinted form as the structure for the conference. The form varies slightly from funeral home to funeral home, but generally includes three main sections: 1. Vital statistics for the death certificate; 2. Obituary information; 3. Service information.

Because this form guides the arrangement conference and because so many "paperwork" details need to be attended to, the session often ends up feeling sterile and clerical. Yes, the funeral director has achieved his necessary goal of gathering vital information, but the family is often not given ample opportunity to focus on the most important goal: planning a healing, meaningful funeral Experience that honors the person who died.

I propose a new process for funeral arranging. This arrangement process focuses on the person who died and the people who loved him with the goal of creating a personalized, meaningful funeral. What was once strictly a data-gathering business meeting becomes a life-affirming, life-honoring creative Experience. The new customer, whom we know to be skeptical of the funeral and the funeral director's role, should leave this new arrangement conference feeling both empowered and enthusiastic about the creation of a personalized funeral.

Step 1: THE INTRODUCTION

During this phase of the arrangement conference (which is often best completed at the family's home and not at the funeral home), the funeral director introduces himself and greets each of the family members in attendance, taking care to understand who each person is and their relationship to the person who died. He also:

- ensures everyone's comfort by offering beverages,kleenex, etc.

- summarizes his role in the funeral planning process.
- emphasizes the importance of planning a personalized, meaningful funeral.
- reviews goals for the arrangement conference:

   1. learn about the family and the person who died.
   2. help the family understand the many opportunities
      they have to both celebrate and mourn the life.
   3. make decisions about these opportunities and create a written
      plan—a script for the staging of a meaningful funeral Experience.

Step 2: GATHERING MEMORIES

During this phase of the arrangement conference, the funeral director acts as biographer, asking questions/stimulating conversation about the life of the person who died and recording the family's responses. He might say, "The best way for me to help you honor _____'s life is to help me understand what he was like, what his life was like. So I'd like to start by asking some general questions about him."

A good way to begin might be to ask an open-ended, very general question, such as "Tell me about _____ (name of person who died) and what kind of person he was." This question will automatically bring to the forefront the most important aspects of the person's life—those aspects that should somehow be honored during the funeral.

Other open-ended follow-up questions might include: "Who was most important to _____?" "Tell me about his early years." "Did he have any hobbies or passions?"

As the family talks, the funeral director fills in the arrangement form. If the family mentions that the person who died was a veteran, for example, the funeral director takes this opportunity to ask the family which branch of the service he was in, what rank he attained, etc. When the family naturally mentions the place of birth and parent and sibling names, the funeral director fills in these blanks.

If the funeral director allows the family to "tell the story," many of the facts of the person's life will naturally unfold. Most important, the family will be talking about the "important" things instead of the facts dictated by the arrangement form. To be avoided during this phase is the typical "Name, date of birth, social security number, etc." question and answer volley.

As Step 2 naturally winds to a close, the funeral director thanks the family for sharing _____'s life with him then suggests a short break. After the break, the funeral director and the family will talk about honoring all the memories they've gathered as part of the ceremony. The funeral director might use the break to peruse his forms and note questions that still need to be answered.

Step 3: PLANNING THE SERVICE

The funeral director begins this phase by teaching the family about the funeral ceremony. The new customer needs to be educated about both the purposes and elements of ceremony. In addition, if something is written down it creates more value. The following hand-outs might be presented and briefly reviewed:

- PURPOSES OF THE FUNERAL CEREMONY
- THE ELEMENTS OF FUNERAL CEREMONIES

This is a good time for the funeral director to determine what sort of funeral ceremony the family has in mind (if he hasn't already determined this naturally through the course of the conversation). Many families will want to work with a certain church or even a certain clergy member at a certain church. The funeral director will then know what opportunities (or limitations) will be imposed on this ceremony and, when possible, can act as liaison and advocate between the family and the clergy—always with an eye to creating a ceremony that will be healing for the family.

At this point the funeral director asks the family whether they've given thought to the how/if they might use the various elements of ceremony. Again, if the family expresses strong likes or dislikes, the funeral director should honor those feelings. If not, he can lead them, step by step, through a discussion of each element:

- the visitation
- open or closed casket
- the funeral ceremony
  - eulogy
  - music
  - symbols
  - memories
- the procession
- the committal service
- burial, cremation or entombment
- the gathering

In cases where the family will rely heavily on a religious leader in planning and carrying out a funeral, the funeral director will have less influence on many aspects of the funeral. However, always mindful of cultural and religious rules about such things, he can still encourage the family to have a visitation (whether public or private), present the benefits of open casket, encourage the family to have a procession if there will be a committal service, and offer his facilities for the gathering. In short, the funeral director still has great influence over many elements of even the most liturgical church funeral and should help the family make the most of them.

But perhaps the funeral director's most important role during this phase of the arrangement conference is to offer the family opportunities to honor the memories they spoke about during Step 2. The family has spoken about the events in the person's life that were most significant. They have shared stories of the people who loved the person who died. The funeral director should ensure that the family considers including important memories and people in the ceremony somehow.

The funeral director might suggest (and show samples or photo examples where possible):

- asking several people to share memories during the funeral
- memory tables
- memory boards
- memory books or boxes
- memory baskets
- memory drawer
- memorial videotapes or slide shows.

In addition, music can be personalized (e.g. jazz played softly in the background at a jazz lover's visitation). The symbols used during the ceremony can be somewhat personalized (e.g. favorite flowers of the person who died). The eulogy can be highly personalized if the person delivering the eulogy is willing to gather the information. And the many people who loved the person who died can be included in the ceremony by being asked to share memories, be pallbearers, play music, etc.

The helpful funeral director should suggest that the funeral home can help coordinate any or all of these memory ideas.

By the end of Step 3, the family and the funeral director should both have a good understanding of when and where the funeral will take place and what the funeral for this person will look like. Most of the details will have been addressed and the family should feel that the funeral director has helped them focus on creating a personalized, unique funeral that will be meaningful to their family.

Step 4: CREATING AN ACTION PLAN AND SUMMARY

It's time for the family to wrap up the arrangement conference now. As required, the funeral director presents the family with a pricing list and goes over the costs that would be incurred if the service they had just planned were carried out.

Casket or urn selection may take place at this time, as well.

Finally, the funeral director makes a copy of the funeral service form he has filled out and presents it to the family along with a list of things still to do.

The family leaves the arrangement conference probably feeling tired but also satisfied that they have worked hard to plan a ceremony befitting the life of the person who died.

Of course, I realize that the arranging process I envision won't work for all families in all circumstances. Not all families will want to share so much about the person who died. Some families will be too upset to open up in this way. Sometimes there may not be time for this process.

But the heart of this arranging process—learning about the person who died—can be applied to some degree to your current arrangement process. The next time you sit down with a new family, before you even begin filling out forms, ask them to tell you about the person who died—and see what happens. This one little question can go a long way to transforming the arrangement conference into an important part of the Experience.

John Horan of Horan & McConaty Funeral Homes in Denver is a good arranger. He begins every funeral arrangement with his file closed and his eyes up. After greeting everyone and providing refreshments, he gives a brief overview of the things that will need to be covered during the meeting. He also discloses that they will spend about two hours together. Then, and here is the key moment, he says something like, "It really helps me do my job well if I'm able to know something about your husband or father. Would it be OK if I asked a few questions?"

To discern the uniqueness of the person who died and to honor the relationships of this person to the living, John tries to ask six questions:

1. Can you tell me something about what happened? (In other words, John invites them to "tell the story.")

2. What sort of work did Mr._____ do? (For a child, he uses the first name and asks about school and activities.)

3. What kinds of things did he like to do?

4. Was he involved in a church or was he spiritual?

5. Have you ever been to a funeral and something took place that seemed just right?

6. Have you ever been to a funeral and experienced something you though was inappropriate?

This line of questioning is meant to lead to ideas that help establish meaning and significance. John also reports that taking the first half hour or so to ask these questions while actively listening and exploring responses creates a special bond between him and the family.

"I hold back from making suggestions about personalizing the ceremony until I've listened carefully to all the responses," says John. "To do otherwise could derail the conversation and result in missed opportunities.

"As funeral directors see increasing numbers of people without ties to religious or cultural traditions and little or no experience with funerals, my role has expanded," John concludes. "The cards, letters and kind words from those we serve testify to the importance of what we do when we elevate our role to that of facilitator and caregiver."

Attitude

A very successful funeral director friend of mine makes a point of greeting other funeral directors he meets with the following: "Isn't it an honor to be in funeral service!" He does this, in part, to set a tone for both himself and his fellow funeral directors. His attitude is genuine and he is someone who makes you feel great about the future of funeral service. Families he works with feel his passion and come to understand he is truly committed to helping them create meaningful funeral Experiences.

Do an inventory check on your attitude. How does your attitude influence your general presence with families you serve and your co-workers? A simple truism is that people feel better in the presence of people who project a positive attitude. If you have anyone on your staff who is projecting negativity on a chronic basis, odds are they will poison other staff members and impact the morale of the entire funeral home.

Owners and managers, especially, have a responsibility to maintain a positive attitude. Your staff can enthusiastically plan engaging, memorable Experiences for families only if you're the most enthusiastic one among them.

My own belief is that customer service in funeral homes should be built upon an attitude of GRATITUDE. This means living out your passion for service. Staff members who possess an attitude of gratitude automatically find ways to deliver better service to families served.

Of course, the opposite of an attitude of gratitude would be a staff person who demonstrates a lack of concern or appreciation for a family's decision to use your funeral home. I was recently presenting an in-service training to a funeral home staff when one of the participants asked, "So, are you suggesting that we be nice to each and every family we serve?" Without hesitation I responded, "No, just the families you ever want to serve again." Sad to say, there are still some people in funeral service who do not understand what a privilege it is to serve families.

In sum, whatever you feel on the inside usually shows on the outside. If you or anyone on staff feels families are an interruption or aggravation, you will unknowingly pass that feeling on to the customer. In contrast, if you start with an attitude that the family you are serving (or will serve, in the case of pre-need) is a valuable asset to your funeral home—essential to your future—you will find ways to honor that.

If you want to provide value-added service to families, you will find ways to make it happen. Your attitude of gratitude will drive your actions. If you genuinely respect and appreciate the families you serve, your behavior will reflect it.

Balance

Does it ever seem that balance is inaccessible to you? Does it ever seem that your life is in overdrive? Do you ever say you want more down-time, yet can't sit still, even for a moment? Does it ever feel like you have too many commitments, too many activities, too much hurry in your daily life?

If you have answered yes to some or all of the above questions, you are not alone. Many in funeral service cram their days with commitments, believing each one of them is necessary. Despite your best efforts to keep your life in balance, and despite the many time-saving tools intended to make your life easier, you are "at-risk" for being out-of-balance.

Part of the problem may be that you have come to believe that balance is foe, not friend. After all, traditional wisdom has taught you that the desire for excellence in the workplace requires dedication beyond the call of duty. For some, the virtues of excellence are defined only in one narrow hallway of life; everything else in life comes after one's work. In fact, should you question this total dedication to work you may be distrusted and not considered part of the "team."

Now, don't get me wrong—I'm not advocating for mediocrity. However, if you only focus on excellence in your work-life as you neglect other areas of your life, you may self-destruct. We all know of funeral directors who have achieved "career success" only to suffer miserably in other important areas of personal life, family life and spiritual life.

I hope that you accept the premise that balance is important to a joyful life. Of course, your use of time is the key to a balanced life. Time cannot be borrowed or stretched. It is in apportioning our time that balance and priorities become vital. When you combine your use of time with your responsibilities and goals, you have some priority decisions to make.

The good news is that if you can slow yourself down and achieve more life-balance, your perception of the entire world will change. You will work smarter, not harder. You will literally breathe easier. You will be able to set priorities in your life in a more effective way. As opposed to waiting to enjoy your life when everything is done (which, of course, it never will be), you can begin to enjoy the journey instead of the destination.

Body

Today's families too often equate funeral service with body disposition, and as we're all well aware, there are many alternative providers helping families dispose of bodies simply, efficiently and inexpensively. A challenge for funeral service, then, is to make the Experience of the funeral more important than the means of disposition.

This is not to say that the body of the person who died isn't important and doesn't demand respect and attention. In fact, today's customer—particularly body burial customers—continue to want to spend time with the body. According to the 2000 Wirthlin Study of American Attitudes Toward Ritualization and Memorialization, 74% of those who had arranged a funeral or cremation for a friend or relative chose to have an open casket for the general public—up significantly from 68% in 1995. That's great news! After all, as you well know, viewing and spending time with the body is a critical step toward reconciling loss for many mourners.

On the other hand, cremation-only customers are less likely to ask for visitation. A recent Options by Batesville study found that 61% of Americans who had arranged a cremation believe there is no need to view the body with cremation. (I think they're wrong, and innovations such as Anderson-McQueen's Cremation Tribute Center (see Cremation) may be changing this perception.)

So, some of today's families will continue to ask for visitation and some will not. But all should be given the option of at least spending some private family time with the body.

Seeing the body encourages mourners to confront the reality and the finality of the death and allows for last goodbyes and visual confirmation that someone loved is indeed dead. In generations past, the body often served as the very locus of mourning; the bereaved came to the dead person's home to view the body, pay their last respects and support the primary mourners. In fact, the body was often displayed for days before burial.

For mourners, to be invited to see the body is to be invited to say goodbye and to touch one last time that person they loved so much. It is also to be invited to confront our disbelief that someone we cared deeply about is gone and cannot return. Far from being morbid or carnivalesque, open casket private time and public services help us acknowledge the reality of the death and transition from life as it was to life as it is now.

Good embalming makes spending time with the body a better Experience for families. Taking a few extra minutes to ensure that features, hair, cosmetics, dressing and placement are as attractive and lifelike as possible can make all the difference. Families may appreciate all you do for them and be generally satisfied with the funeral Experience, but if the body presentation is less than satisfactory, you'll probably never see that family again.

Remember the Escapist realm of experience from Chapter 3? Inviting families to do something, to participate in preparing the body, is a good idea for some. Family members can comb or style hair, dress the body, apply nail polish or make-up. Simply stroking the hand or hair of the person who died makes spending time with the body more of a meaningful Experience. Let families know it's OK to touch, but do explain beforehand what the person's skin will feel like.

Of course, we must respect cultural and religious differences concerning the treatment of and focus on the body. Judaism, for example, prohibits embalming or any cosmetic "restoration." Viewing of the body is seen as a violation of the rights of the dead.

Burnout

What happens when funeral directors repeatedly ignore their own needs? Sometimes, influences such as bereavement overload (experiencing overwhelming loss within a short time span or, in this case, being around loss too much), unrealistic expectations about helping all the bereaved families in one's community or discovering that, at times, one cares more about others than they care about themselves, results in what I call "funeral director fatigue syndrome."

Symptoms of this syndrome often include the following:

- exhaustion and loss of energy
- irritability and impatience
- cynicism and detachment
- physical complaints and depression
- disorientation and confusion
- feelings of omnipotence and indispensability
- minimization and denial of feelings

Let's examine each of these stress-related symptoms and then explore ways in which you can strive to take care of yourself in the face of these symptoms.

Exhaustion and loss of energy

Feelings of exhaustion and loss of energy are usually among the first signals of funeral director distress. For many, low energy and fatigue can be difficult to acknowledge because they are the opposite of the high energy level required to meet funeral home demands.

Our bodies are powerful instruments and frequently wiser than our minds. Exhaustion and lack of physical and psychic energy are often unconscious "cries for self help." If we could only slow down and listen to the voice within.

Irritability and impatience

Irritability and impatience are inherent to the experience of funeral director burnout. As effective helpers we typically feel a sense of accomplishment and reward for our efforts. As stress increases, however, our ability to feel reward diminishes while our irritability and impatience become heightened.

Disagreements and tendencies to blame others for interpersonal difficulties may occur as stress takes its toll on your sense of emotional and physical well-being. A real sign to watch for: You have more compassion and sensitivity for those you work with than you have for your own family.

Cynicism and detachment

As funeral directors experiencing emotional burn-out, you may begin to respond to stress in a manner that saves something of yourself. You may begin to question the value of helping others, of your family life, of friendships, even of life itself. You may work to convince yourself that "there's no point in getting involved" as you rationalize your need to distance yourself from the stress of interpersonal encounters.

Detachment serves to help distance you from feelings of pain, helplessness and hurt. I have also observed that a general sense of impatience with those we care for often goes hand-in-hand with cynicism and detachment.

Physical complaints and depression

Physical complaints, real or imagined, are often experienced by funeral directors suffering from fatigue syndrome. Sometimes, physical complaints are easier for us to talk about than emotional concerns. The process of consciously or unconsciously converting emotional conflicts may result in a variety of somatic symptoms like headaches, stomachaches, backaches and long-lasting colds.

Generalized feelings of depression are also common to the phenomenon of funeral director burnout. Loss of appetite, difficulty sleeping, sudden changes in mood and lethargy suggest that depression has become a part of the overall stress syndrome. Depression is a constellation of symptoms that together tell us something is wrong, and that we must pay attention and try to understand.

Disorientation and confusion

Feelings of disorientation and confusion are often experienced as a component of this syndrome. Your mind may shift from one topic to another and focusing on current tasks often becomes difficult. You may experience "polyphasic behavior," whereby you feel busy, yet not accomplish much at all. Since difficulty focusing results in a lack of a personal sense of competence, confusion only results in more heightened feelings of disorientation.

Thus, a cycle of confusion resulting in disorientation evolves and becomes difficult to break. The ability to think clearly suffers and concentration and memory are impaired. In addition, the ability to make decisions and sound judgments becomes limited. Obviously, your system is overloaded and in need of a break from the continuing cycle of stress.

Omnipotence and indispensability

Another common symptom of funeral director fatigue syndrome is a sense of omnipotence and indispensability. Statements like, "No one else can provide the kind of care I can," or, "I have got to be the one to help these families" are not simply the expressions of a healthy ego.

Other people can provide care to bereaved families and many do it very well. When we as caregivers begin to feel indispensable, we tend to block not only our own growth, but the growth and healing of others.

Minimization and denial of feelings

When stressed to their limits, some funeral directors continue to minimize, if not out-and-out deny, feelings of burnout. The funeral director who minimizes is aware of feeling stressed, but works to minimize these feelings by diluting them through a variety of rationalizations. From a self-perspective, minimizing stress seems to work, particularly because it is commensurate with the self-imposed principle of "being all things to all people." However, internally repressed feelings of stress build within and emotional strain results.

Perhaps the most dangerous characteristic of funeral director fatigue syndrome is the total denial of feelings of stress. As denial takes over, the funeral director's symptoms of stress become enemies to be fought instead of friends to be understood. Regardless of how loud the mind and body cry out for relief, no one is listening.

Emotional Involvement and Stress

The reasons funeral directors feel stress are often multiple and complex. When we care deeply for people in grief, we open ourselves to our own vulnerabilities related to loss issues. Perhaps another person's grief stimulates memories of some old griefs of our own. Perhaps those we wish to help frustrate our efforts to be supportive.

Whatever the reason, the natural way to prevent ourselves from being hurt or disappointed is to deny feelings in general. The denial of feelings is often accompanied by an internal sense of a lack of purpose. After all, the willingness and ability to feel are ultimately what gives meaning to life.

Of all the stresses death caregivers are subject to, emotional involvement appears central to the potential of suffering from this syndrome. Perhaps we should ask ourselves what we lose when we decide to minimize or ignore the significant level of emotional involvement intrinsic to caring for bereaved families. We probably will discover that in the process of minimizing or ignoring, we are, in fact, eliminating our potential to help people move toward a sense of inner peace. As the saying goes, "If you want to help others, the place to start is with yourself."

We probably need to remind ourselves that we are our own most important helping instrument and that what we know about ourselves makes a tremendous difference in our capacity to assist others. While the admirable goal of helping bereaved families may alone seem to justify emotional sacrifices, ultimately we are not helping others effectively when we ignore what we are experiencing within ourselves.

Obviously, we cannot draw close to others without beginning to affect and be affected by them. This is the nature of the helping relationship with those confronting death. We cannot help others from a protective position. Helping occurs openly where we are defenseless—if we allow ourselves to be. My experience suggests it takes practice to work toward an understanding of what is taking place inside oneself, while trying to grasp what it taking place inside others. After all, these thoughts and feelings occur simultaneously and are significantly interrelated.

Involving yourself with others, particularly at a time of death and grief, requires taking care of yourself as well as others. Emotional overload, circumstances surrounding death, and caring about the bereaved will unavoidably result in times of funeral director fatigue syndrome. When this occurs, you should feel no sense of inadequacy or stigma if you also need the support and understanding of others.

Am I experiencing funeral director fatigue syndrome?

A funeral director recently asked me, "How is burnout different from stress?" We might overhear a staff person comment, "I'm really feeling burned out today." All of us may have occasional days when our motivation and energy levels are low. While this fluctuation in energy states is normal, burnout is an end stage that typically develops over time. Once a person is burned out, dramatic changes are necessary to reverse the process.

Psychologist Christina Maslach, a leading authority on burnout, has outlined three major signs of burnout (what I'm calling funeral director fatigue syndrome):

- Emotional exhaustion—feeling drained, not having anything to give even before the day begins.

- Depersonalization—feeling disconnected from other people, feeling resentful and seeing them negatively.

- Reduced sense of personal accomplishment—feeling ineffective, that the results achieved are not meaningful.

Step back for a moment and complete the following brief fatigue syndrome survey. As you review your life over the past twelve months, answer the survey questions:

Funeral director fatigue syndrome survey

1. Do you generally feel fatigued and lacking in energy?

2. Are you getting irritable, impatient and angry with people around you (home and/or work)?

3. Do you feel cynical toward and detached from the families you serve?

4. Do you suffer from more than your share of physical complaints, such as headaches, stomachaches, backaches and long-lasting colds?

5. Do you generally feel depressed or notice sudden fluctuations in your moods?

6. Do you feel busy, yet have a sense that you don't accomplish much at all?

7. Do you have difficulty concentrating or remembering?

8. Do you think you have to be the one to help all bereaved families that come through your door?

9. Do you feel less of a sense of satisfaction about your helping efforts than you have in the past?

10. Do you feel that you just don't have anything more to give?

In general, if you answered "yes" to 2-4 of these questions, you may be in the early phases of funeral director fatigue syndrome. If you answered "yes" to 5-7 of these questions, you are quickly moving in the direction of total fatigue. If you answered "yes" to 8-10 of these questions, you are burned out!

Change

We all know that funeral service has become more competitive and complex in recent years and that you need to keep up with these changes if your company is to prosper.

Actually, you need to do more than "keep up." To enjoy ongoing success, funeral homes must grab change by the tail and tame it. Only a proactive, take-charge response to change will result in customer satisfaction and continued growth.

How is your funeral home responding to change?

1) "We'd better cover our behind!": The Reactionary Response

An OSHA inspector knocks on your door and finds you haven't met the standards of the latest ruling. A family whose son just died of AIDS calls for your services, and you have no AIDS protocol in place. What do you do? You REACT, often sloppily, to cover your behind.

Could these scenarios have been prevented? Probably. Funeral directors who look ahead and anticipate change can circumvent most crises. When funeral homes are reactionary, on the other hand, they pay the price—in both dollars and consumer confidence. In fact, some funeral homes have "reactionaried" themselves right out of business.

2) "Keeping up with the Joneses": The Evolutionary Response

The evolutionary response to change is when you slowly adapt by following the lead of others. Instead of envisioning your own future, you let others create that future for you.

Perhaps the most classic example of the evolutionary response to change has been in the area of pre-need. Many funeral homes entered the pre-need marketplace only after they saw the consequences of *not* doing so. Another example: the

FTC ruling on itemized pricing. Some funeral homes were putting the bulk of their profit in the casket and didn't know how they arrived at their service fee. They slowly changed their fee structures, but by the time they finally figured it out, they had lost untold dollars.

The cost of the evolutionary response to change is the cost of lost opportunity. And lost opportunities can mean lost customers. Perhaps Will Rogers said it best, "Even if you are on the right track, if you just sit there you are going to get run over."

3) "Just do it": The Proactive Response

Being proactive means anticipating change and acting ahead of time to make the most of that change. As management consultant Peter Drucker has said, "The best way to predict the future is to create it."

Being proactive starts with analyzing your customers' present and future needs and the trends or "new rules" of surviving in funeral service, and then implementing the necessary and prudent management changes.

Being proactive means continually asking yourself the following questions: How are the needs of our customers changing? What are the new rules of surviving and succeeding in funeral service? What changes do we need to make right now? What actions can we take that will add value to our services? What can we do to position ourselves as different from (and more valuable than) other funeral homes in our service area? What can we do to create better Experiences for families?

Take whatever downtime you need to—no interruptions—to ask yourself these questions. The answers you discover may not call for a complete overhaul in your business practices, but even proactive fine-tuning will put you ten steps ahead.

Children

Children are a unique and very important group of funeral home "customers." The impressions they form of funerals during their tender years will stay with them throughout their lives. They are the funeral home customers of the future. They are also an important part of every family who walks through your door. Making sure that their funeral Experiences are positive and healing should be a special focus at every funeral home.

Following are some guidelines for working with children at the time of a death.

Talking to children about death

1) *Don't use euphemisms.* For example, saying a dead person is "asleep" will not only mislead a child, but may also cause her to believe that the dead person might "wake up" again. Remember, children can cope with what they know. They cannot cope with what they don't know.

2) *Use simple, concrete language.* Young children are very literal. Try not to use abstract or complex words.

3) *Don't over-explain.* While children deserve developmentally-appropriate explanations about death, they don't need *War and Peace*. Be brief. Let the child's natural curiosity—not your need to be understood—guide your discussions.

4) *Show them.* Children often don't understand something until they can see it. You will not harm them, for example, by showing them the ashes from a cremation or taking them to the funeral home to look at caskets.

Explaining funeral terms

Ashes (also "cremains")	What is left of a dead body after cremation. Looks like ashes from a fire.
Burial	Placing the body (which is inside a casket or an urn) into the ground.

Calling hours (also "visitation" or "wake")	The times that are set for people to come visit the family and view the body before the funeral service.
Casket	A special box for burying a dead body.
Cemetery	A place where many dead bodies are buried.
Committal service	The part of the funeral service that takes place where the body will be buried. Includes burial.
Cremation	Putting the dead body into a room with lots of heat until it turns into ashes.
Dead	When a person's body stops working. It doesn't see, hear, feel, eat, breathe, etc. anymore. The person can never come back.
Embalm	When the funeral home gets the body ready to put in the casket so we can see the body at the viewing. (While you may be tempted to talk about taking all of the blood out and putting a special chemical in, this is most often an example of overexplanation to young children. Of course, if the child asks, then you can explain.)
Funeral	A time when friends and families get together to say goodbye and remember the person who died. May be held at the funeral home or the church.
Funeral director	A person who works at the funeral home and helps the family plan the funeral.
Funeral home	A place where bodies are kept until they are buried. Sometimes the funeral is also held at the funeral home.
Grave	The hole in the ground where the body is buried at the cemetery.
Headstone or monument	A stone placed at the grave that marks where the person who died is buried.
Hearse (also "funeral coach")	The special car that takes the dead body in the casket to the grave at the cemetery.

Mausoleum	A special building in which bodies can be buried above the ground.
Obituary	A short article in the paper that tells about the person who died.
Pallbearer	The people who help carry the casket at the funeral.
Plot	The area of ground at the cemetery where the body will be buried.
Urn	A small container that the ashes are placed in after cremation.
Vault	An outside box that the casket is put in for burial. (Note for adults: Many cemeteries require vaults because they prevent the ground above the casket from sinking.)
Viewing (also "wake" or "calling hours")	The time when people can see the body of the person who died.

Causes of death

Accident	Something really awful happened. (Explain the nature of the accident.) The person's body was hurt so badly that it stopped working.
Homicide	Sometimes a person whose mind is not working right kills another person. That is the worst thing a person can do in this world; it is wrong and can make us very mad.
Miscarriage/stillbirth	Sometimes when a baby is growing inside its mommy, something goes wrong. We don't always understand why it happens, but it's nobody's fault.
Old age	When people have lived a long, long time and get very old, their bodies wear out and eventually stop working.
Sudden Infant Death Syndrome (SIDS)	Sometimes, not very often, little babies die in their sleep. Nobody knows for sure why it

	happens. It didn't happen because of any thing anybody did or didn't do.
Suicide	Sometimes people feel very sad and don't want to live anymore so they kill themselves. Isn't that a shame? What else could the person who was feeling bad do to help himself feel better? *(Inititate a discussion on reaching out for help.)*
Terminal illness	Sometimes when people get sick, they don't get better. Instead, they get sicker and sicker until their bodies wear out and eventually stop working.

Keep in mind that these suggested explanations are not meant to be used verbatim. Use language that you feel comfortable with and that you think will make sense to the particular child you're helping.

Explaining Cremation to Children

If there is one rule of thumb to keep in mind as you guide this child through the funeral Experience, it is this: Follow the child's lead. If you listen to her and pay attention to her behaviors, the child will teach you what she is curious about, what doesn't interest her, what makes her scared.

Follow her lead as you answer her questions about cremation. Give her only as much information as she wants to know. If she has more questions, she'll probably ask—especially if you've shown her that you are someone who will answer her questions honestly and openly.

Whatever information you and the family choose to share with the grieving child, take care to use words that he will understand. This depends not only on the child's age, but also his developmental level, his personality and his vocabulary. If your words and your tone convey that you are comfortable with the process of cremation, the child will likely feel the same way.

Think twice before withholding all information about cremation from children. Some would say that cremation is too violent a process to explain to children, yet children can cope with what they know. They cannot cope with what they don't know or have never been told. Often their imaginations can conjure up explanations much scarier than reality.

Also be careful about using euphemisms or even fibbing to children in an attempt to protect them from the truth. For example, if a child is told that God took the person to heaven yet the adults around her are all talking about something called cremation or ashes, she may well become more confused and upset than she would have been if a compassionate adult gently told her the truth.

Some Child-Friendly Cremation Information

- There is no smell and no smoke when a body is cremated. It just gets very hot—about three times as hot as your oven at home can get. The heat burns away all the parts of the body except some pieces of bone.

- After cremation, what's left of the body looks like fishbowl rocks or kitty litter, except it's white because it's bone. It's put in a clear plastic bag so you can see it if you want to.

- When a dead body is buried in the ground, it breaks down after months and years and just a skeleton is left. Cremation makes this happen much, much faster.

- Cremation has been used for thousands of years. The ancient Greeks and Romans built funeral pyres (rhymes with hires), which were stacks of wood the body was put on top of. The wood was set afire and the body burned, too. Funeral pyres are still used in India today.

- Cremation doesn't hurt. The person is dead, which means the body doesn't work any more. Its heart doesn't beat, its brain has stopped working, it doesn't breathe and it doesn't feel anything anymore.

- The people doing the cremation take it very seriously and handle the body with a lot of respect. Just like you do, they understand that _____ (the person who died) was a unique, special person who deserves to leave this world with dignity.

Helping Children with Funerals and Helping Children Understand Cremation are published in brochure form to make available to families served. For sample copies, call the Center for Loss at (970) 226-6050.

Committals

The burial of the body or the urn, the witnessing of the body's committal to the cremation chamber and the scattering of ashes not only help families acknowledge the reality and finality of the death, they also symbolize the separation that the death has created. Participating in a committal definitely enhances the funeral Experience. I always encourage families to have committal services when at all possible and appropriate and I hope you do the same.

It should also be noted that some families choose to have only a committal service, without visitation and/or a funeral or memorial service. While I strongly believe that families should be encouraged to make use of as many elements of ritual as possible, you must also honor their choice when they settle on "committal only." In these cases it is particularly important that you do everything in your power to make the committal a meaningful Experience.

To make the most of the committal Experience, create a service that includes the actual lowering of the casket or urn into the ground. I realize that this can be a hassle and that not all cemeteries will accommodate this request, but when possible it is a truly healing experience. Have mourners throw handsful of dirt or flowers into the gravesite. You can also suggest that families observe a moment of silence in which each person thinks about their unique memories of the person who died. At the close of the committal or scattering, a spiritual passage, quotation or poem is appropriate. Because they are spoken last in the funeral process, the committal words may be those that families remember best.

Committals and scatterings are also appropriate times for personalized music, personalized readings and brief memory sharing. Live music, perhaps bagpipes or a guitar or trumpets, truly enhances the committal and makes it memorable and healing for all in attendance.

Don't forget to verbally invite and encourage everyone to attend the gathering as soon as the committal is over. Print up directions to the gathering's location and hand them out as people leave the committal.

Communication

Funeral director-family communication can be seen as an exchange between two or more people. And, actually, three very different, yet interdependent levels of communication exist.

The three levels we will identify and describe are:

1. the exchange of information;
2. the exchange of emotion; and
3. the exchange of meaning.

The exchange of information involves the funeral director obtaining essential factual information from the family, i.e., social security number, veteran's information, etc. While this process may seem simple, this exchange is complicated by the reality that humans do not give and receive information passively. Emotions—particularly when heightened by grief—color everything. So, it's never as simple as just asking questions and getting answers.

You are working with people in acute grief who will be very sensitive to your capacity to empathize and "be with" them. If the family senses interpersonal distance or a funeral director who just wants information so he or she can "get the job done," they will consciously or unconsciously pull away from the interaction. A constant awareness of people's feelings must be an integral part of the funeral director's helping role.

Finally, an exchange of meaning occurs. The family comes to you to create a funeral that will bring them meaning and purpose. As you communicate with them, they "teach you" how you can help them create a meaningful funeral service. This means going beyond surface communication to seeking an understanding of how you can aid them in their "search for meaning." If they go away from the funeral without a sense of meaning or value, odds are they won't come back to you for service in the future.

The successful funeral director-family encounter consists of all three of these levels of communication. Awareness of these levels will allow you to stay conscious of how they impact your interactions with families served.

Communication Don'ts

To effectively deliver customer service, funeral directors must empathetically understand (and be understood by) the families they serve. They must also be aware of the following destructive communication patterns:

Dominating the conversation

The person who dominates an interaction with another person generally exudes a general sense of impatience, may change the subject or attempt to persuade or coerce and (probably unbeknownst to him) is often thought of as lecturing or preaching.

The "dominator" often thinks she knows the answer before the question is even posed. She thinks she knows exactly what people should do and likes to tell them when and how to do it. This person is often a very poor listener.

Be on the watch for dominating behaviors in your communication patterns, for they communicate a sense of disrespect for your customers' thoughts and feelings.

Bombarding with questions

Let me reemphasize here that the excessive use of questions tends to limit interactions with the families you serve. Relying largely on closed-ended questions to gain information and understand feelings is destructive in that you, as opposed to the bereaved family you are helping, steer the conversation and in doing so cover only what you perceive is important.

The "bombarder" might run off a series of questions like, "What was your father's date of birth? Where was he born? What was his social security number? Was he a veteran?" This approach usually makes the bereaved family feel like you are just filling out forms instead of truly trying to understand their unique feelings and needs. In addition, this pattern of interaction is usually difficult to change. If early in the conversation you assume a strong directive role characterized by excessive questioning, the bereaved family may consider this the expected situation and adopt a passive role.

Inappropriate self-disclosing

The "self-discloser" has been known to bore people to death. He likes to talk about himself, particularly personal experiences. This funeral director might say to bereaved families something like, "When my grandfather died we decided it would be best to..."

Remember that talking at length about oneself draws the focus away from the family you are attempting to help. Chances are slim that the family will find such anecdotes relevant to their situation. Self-disclosure can be appropriate on occasion; however, in general, the best procedure is to keep the focus of your helping efforts on those you are assisting.

Offering platitudes or false reassurance

To offer false reassurance is to distance yourself from the family you are attempting to help. When someone has experienced the death of someone loved, false reassurance often leaves feelings of loneliness, misunderstanding and emptiness. The platitude-offerer often speaks in clichés like, "Time heals all wounds," "Everything is going to be just fine," or "Hang in there." These kinds of statements almost always fail to provide the reassurance intended. Instead, the person whose feelings do not agree with such comments is convinced that you certainly do not understand.

Funeral directors who feel compelled to offer platitudes or false reassurance seem to think they can make someone's grief just go away. But again, this pattern of communication is not respectful because it does not take into consideration the bereaved family's understanding of the way things are. You will be better off exploring painful realities than to communicate an attitude of false reassurance.

Discouraging the expression of emotions and tears

Unfortunately, many people associate tears of grief with personal inadequacy and weakness. Crying on the part of the mourner often generates feelings of helplessness in friends, family and caregivers. Funeral directors are not immune from this tendency, either.

Out of a wish to protect the mourner from pain, those people surrounding the mourner may try to discourage tears. Comments like, "Tears won't bring him back," and "He wouldn't want you to cry" do inhibit the expression of tears, yet crying is nature's way of releasing internal tension in the body and allowing the mourner to communicate a need to be comforted.

Becoming a helping funeral director means making a commitment to allowing people to share their pain with you. Obviously, you cannot and should not try to discourage whatever emotions the bereaved families you serve may be experiencing.

Emotional distancing

Distancing can occur in helping relationships in different ways. Literal detachment occurs when you simply perform the required tasks while maintaining a sense of personal aloofness and distance. In this situation, the bereaved families in your care will probably feel isolated and sense a lack of warmth and caring.

Another form of detachment is to avoid discussion of painful issues. This is often done in an effort to protect the family you are helping—and yourself—from confronting the reality of the feelings. In actuality, healing can only occur if these painful feelings are expressed.

Competition

As I travel North America as a death educator and consultant to funeral service, it's my honor to serve as a listener to my funeral director friends. Recently, I have heard a lot of talk about the "competition."

We all realize that funeral service has changed dramatically in recent years. Yes, you have new competition ranging from casket stores to discount funeral homes to marketers of immediate cremation. In addition, you have a new customer who is questioning the need to participate in funeral ceremonies. Everything about funeral service is changing rapidly.

Sometimes when people experience fear, they get angry. And the natural place to direct one's anger is at the competition. Yet, sometimes so much energy is focused on the competition that you can forget where your true focus needs to be—on those you serve, the families who turn to you when someone dies.

When change is rapid and competition is fierce, it's also easy to want to hold onto "the old ways" of doing things and wish the competition would just go away. As one funeral director recently said to me, "Our instinct in funeral service is to hang on to what we know and not let go. We stick our heads in the sand, tell each other nothing is really changing all that much and bad-mouth the competition. We do this even in the face of massive evidence that the entire nature of funeral service is changing."

His comment brought to mind a metaphor I sometimes use in my teaching. When things around you are changing, imagine yourself as a trapeze artist suspended between trapezes. You've let go of the old trapeze (the old ways of funeral service), and you're waiting—suspended in mid air—for the new trapeze to show up.

Part of holding on to the old trapeze relates to protecting your own turf. It's almost instinctive to respond in frustration and anger toward new competition that has emerged in funeral service. Yet, the more focus you put on the competition, the more tendency you have to drift away from focusing on the families you serve. The combination of massive change and preoccupation with the competition can result in a funeral home's isolation from the very families it serves.

The paradox of change is that you cannot grab the new until you have let go of the old. In a very real sense, those of you in funeral service must allow yourselves to dangle in mid-air, all the time believing that the new trapeze can and will show up. In addition, you must start reaching out and grabbing hold of the new trapeze.

The Future of Funeral Service Requires Focus and Flexibility

As funeral service enters the new millennium, the operative terms will be *focus* and *flexibility*.

Focus relates to the difference between the sun and a laser. The sun showers the earth with billions of kilowatts of energy each day. That's a lot of energy. In contrast, a laser is a weak source of energy. But with a laser you can focus a few watts and drill a hole in a diamond.

When you focus your funeral home, you can create a similar impact. When a funeral home becomes unfocused it loses its power. Are you focusing your funeral home to create the power of a laser or are you trying to outshine the sun? The more you concern yourself with the competition, the less focus you have.

Flexibility relates to its very definition: yielding to influence; readily changed or changing. Is your funeral home yielding to the influence of the customer? Are you hearing what they are telling you and responding accordingly? Is your funeral home hanging on to what you've known and not letting go? Is your funeral home defending the "traditional" funeral as the only correct choice for families?

The Advantages of Focus and Flexibility

The focused and flexible funeral home understands that the new customer will continue to demand more information, more choices and more value than in the past. Those funeral homes that prescribe only traditional funerals, limit family choices and discourage creativity may as well put up a sign out front that reads, "SLOWLY BUT SURELY GOING OUT OF BUSINESS."

The focused and flexible funeral home will have an overall business plan, service strategy, and effective leaders in management positions. As noted management authority Peter Drucker has noted, "The only things that evolve by themselves in an organization are disorder, friction, and malperformance. What is needed are leaders who recognize that change is needed . . . rather than reacting to the inevitable crisis." Operating a funeral home without a defined business plan and service strategy may have worked 25 years ago, but it won't work in the new millennium and with the evolution of the "never-satisfied customer."

The focused and flexible funeral home will listen and respond to the serendipitous ideas that families bring you. For example, one trend we will continue to see is families holding services at places other than the funeral home or place of worship. I predict we will see more and more home-based and outdoor services. Will your funeral home "yield to this influence" or will you resist change as others adapt to the new customer?

The focused and flexible funeral home will create proactive, community-based educational programs about the value of funerals. As "gatekeepers of ceremony," funeral home staffs will outreach into the community and teach about how personalized, meaningful funerals help people integrate loss into their lives.

The focused and flexible funeral home will have the economic mission and the purpose mission in balance. In turbulent times it's tempting to weigh in on the side of the economic mission. Yet, the challenge is to pay attention to the purpose mission, to bring it back into balance. The overall mission of funeral service is to create meaningful funerals for those families you are privileged to serve. If you have passion for what you do and people sense this in your commitment to help them, you will not only survive challenging times, you will thrive and grow economically.

In summary, to achieve focus and flexibility requires that you direct your energy toward those you serve, not your competition. Effectively responding to the rapid changes in funeral service demands maintaining a laser-sharp focus and letting go of the old trapeze!

Cremation

"We want cremation."

Statistical projections suggest that North American funeral directors will continue to hear more and more customers uttering this phrase—36% by the year 2010. While some might want you to believe differently, cremation as a form of disposition is not inherently bad. In fact, used creatively and flexibly, cremation can actually increase a bereaved family's ceremony options.

My concern as a grief counselor, however, is that many families I counsel after a death have chosen cremation with no accompanying funeral ritual. I imagine you share my frustration that many people who come through your door appear to lack an understanding of how meaningful ceremonies can assist in the healing process. For numerous reasons, many people today are not aware of the need to mourn, let alone understand the ways in which funerals begin to meet this need. This makes your role as a funeral director difficult indeed.

Still, as funeral planners, you have the privilege and responsibility to help bereaved family members begin emotional, physical and spiritual healing through meaningful ceremonies. Authentic funerals embrace both constancy and transformation, helping survivors begin to re-center themselves in order to make that painful, but necessary, transition from life before the death to life after the death.

So, how do you respond in a helpful manner to your cremation customers? I believe that a helpful, non-defensive framework to consider can be outlined as INFORMATION-EDUCATION-CHOICES. Of course, we have all encountered some in funeral service who immediately get defensive when the "C" word comes up. You might hear them say, "Well, there's nothing you can do to change their mind, so why bother trying." This self-defeating response assumes people are not open to learning about their cremation options. Yet, as progressive funeral directors realize, many people are very responsive to exploring information that is offered in a compassionate, well-intentioned manner.

You are the empathetic, knowledgeable professional with the expertise to help bereaved families. Present options to families and honor their decisions. Yes, some people will still choose direct cremation and no services. However, if you can companion families through each of these steps—information, education and choices—your funeral home will exist for years into the future. My observation suggests that getting defensive with families who choose cremation will only result in closing yourself off from a large segment of funeral service customers.

Let's explore the ways in which meaningful funeral ceremonies help the bereaved meet mourning needs (a vital component of the information-education-choices model) so that, ultimately, they may reconcile their grief and go on to find continued meaning in life and living. In an ideal world, people you serve would have an awareness of these mourning needs prior to "at need" times. The art is to present information in a caring way, a way that allows the bereaved to better understand why we have had funerals since the beginning of time. Amazingly enough, many people can and do relate to the why of funerals if they pause to give thought to it. You have the honor of helping them consider the value in meaningful funeral Experiences, regardless of the form of disposition.

Mourning Need #1. Acknowledge the reality of the death. Attempt to help cremation customers understand the importance of confronting the reality of the death. Encourage them to spend time with the body before cremation. Offer them the option of a body viewing followed by cremation. (Stay sensitive to cultural differences in the meaning and appropriateness of body viewing, however.) Provide the option of having family members accompany the body to the crematory.

Mourning Need #2. Move toward the pain of the loss. Discourage cremation customers from skipping funeral ceremonies altogether—which many of them are wont to do. Explain to them the importance of having some type of death ritual, particularly one that allows them to confront their pain. Fortunately, meaningful rituals have the capacity to hold contradictions. It's OK to celebrate the life lived while also embracing one's sadness. Some cremation customers need help in understanding that a major purpose of funerals is to allow for sadness.

Mourning Need #3. Remember the person who died. You can help cremation customers remember the person who died by encouraging them to create memorials. Some may want to scatter cremains in a scattering garden or design a special plaque for hanging on a memorial wall. Others may want to plant a tree or create a videotape depicting the life of the dead person. There are a multitude of creative ideas to help cremation customers get this mourning need met.

Mourning Need #4. Develop a new self-identity. The funeral helps us begin this difficult process of developing a new self-identity because it provides a social venue for public acknowledgment of our new roles. If you are a parent of a child and that child dies, the funeral marks the beginning of your life as a *former* parent (in the physical sense; you will always have that relationship through memory). Others attending the funeral are in effect saying, "We acknowledge your changed identity and we want you to know we still care about you." On the other hand, in situations where there is no funeral (most common in conjunction with cremation), the social group does not know how to relate to the person whose identity has changed and often that person is socially abandoned.

Mourning Need #5. Search for meaning. When someone loved dies, we naturally question the meaning of life and death. Why did this person die? Why now? Why this way? What happens after death? Funerals are a way in which we as individuals and as a community convey our beliefs and values about life and death. The very fact of a funeral demonstrates that death is important to us.

Mourning Need #6. Receive ongoing support from others. As we have said, funerals are a public means of expressing our beliefs and feelings about the death of someone loved. In fact, funerals are the public venue for offering support to others and being supported in grief, both at the time of the funeral and into the future. Funerals make a social statement that says, "Come support me." Whether they realize it or not, those who choose not to have a funeral are saying, "Don't come support me."

Please don't let your cremation customers run away from the painful but necessary journey through grief. Remember: Your role is to offer information, education and choices. I challenge you to consider your customers' mourning needs each time you sit down with a new family to plan a funeral.

The Cremation Experience

So how do you provide cremation, create meaningful Experiences for families who choose cremation, *and* make a profit?

Bill McQueen of Anderson-McQueen Funeral Homes in St. Petersburg, Florida has come up with a good answer. He saw his cremation business increasing and wanted to offer his cremation families more meaningful Experiences. What's more, many families were asking if they could visit the crematory and somehow participate in the cremation process. (Remember—Boomers like to take an active part.) As is common, Anderson-McQueen's crematory (co-owned by a consortium of area funeral homes) was located in an industrial park area—hardly the place or the facility to help bereaved families say goodbye to someone loved.

In late 1997, McQueen, his brother John and sister Maggi, who together own and run three family funeral homes in the St. Petersburg area, built a Cremation Tribute Center adjacent to one of their funeral homes. The 6,000 square foot facility includes a 2,000 square foot preparation facility for body storage and embalming. The remainder of the lovely, open-to-the-public building houses a crematory, a Witness Room, a small family conference room and a Gathering Room for visitations and receptions.

The Witness Room is a small ampitheater separated from the crematory by a large glassed wall. Families can sit in the semi-circular, tiered seating and, after saying their last goodbyes to the body, watch the beginning of the cremation process. The Cremation Tribute Center has an automated loading device that loads the casket or cremation container into the crematory, and families can even press the remote control button to begin the cremation process. For regulatory reasons, Anderson-McQueen also requires that all bodies be identified before cremation. Identification often takes place in the Witness Room, and families sometimes stay to watch cremation begin.

Not all families want to see the initiation of the cremation process, but Bill McQueen reports that five or six a month do want to be there and witness the process. It's obviously something that must be meeting a need of theirs to participate. These families really appreciate the opportunity to pay their last respects in a comfortable, aesthetically pleasing facility.

The family conference room is often used for private prayer before a viewing or cremation. The Gathering Room can be used for visitations and funeral ceremonies before cremation or body burial and is used a lot for receptions following a cremation or body burial. The setting is pleasant and comfortable and has kitchenette facilities. Many families have full catered meals there following the funeral. Outside the Gathering Room is a walled Memorial Garden with flowers, piped music and a beautiful tiered fountain.

"The Cremation Tribute Center has shown us that just because you're a cremation family doesn't mean you don't want to gather together, witness the body, have a ceremony or somehow participate in the process," emphasizes McQueen.

By the end of 1999 they had done about 1,100 cremations through the Cremation Tribute Center since it opened. Now they have the premier cremation facility in their service area and are able to offer customers so much added value, they've been able to raise their service charges accordingly. In addition to creating meaning for families in the cremation process, the Cremation Tribute Center has been a tremendous financial success.

Smartly, Anderson-McQueen also has an open door policy for their Cremation Tribute Center. Anyone can stop by at any time they're open for business and be toured through the operational side of the facility as well as the public side. They also advertise and hold a monthly cremation seminar during the winter. The seminar explains the legalities and process of cremation; participants are then toured through the entire building. I'm proud to say that my Honoring Family Choices signage (available from Batesville) helps explain the hows and whys of funerals. About 25-30 people attend this seminar every month.

"The more we can educate the public, the more they'll come to the decision that they're getting the most value for their dollar by coming to us. And we're very proud of this facility. We love to show it off!" exclaims McQueen.

If you'd like to learn more about the Cremation Tribute Center, Anderson-McQueen's phone number is (727) 822-2059. Just ask for Bill. You can also e-mail him at bmcqueen@andersonmcqueen.com.

Details

Some might say that to obsess about details doesn't serve you well. I simply disagree. A meaningful funeral, in essence, is bringing together numerous details in a way that creates a meaningful funeral Experience. The "little details" can make all the difference to a bereaved family.

For example, you can do everything almost perfectly, yet if you get a small detail in the newspaper obituary wrong, some families will decide you messed up the entire service experience.

So, what is my point? My point is that being concerned about details comes with being a responsible funeral home employee. Review the details on a regular basis:

• How are you ensuring that obituary details are accurate?

• How are you ensuring that your sound system and music system are state-of-the-art?

• How are you ensuring your facility is clean?

• How are you ensuring a neat and well-dressed appearance of all of your staff?

• How are you ensuring your automobiles are clean?

And the list goes on and on...

Remember—check details once, twice, three times. Take the "little things" seriously—before they become "big things" with the families you serve.

Donors

Can organ donation be a positive part of the death and funeral Experience for today's families? Absolutely. Many families take great comfort in having donated tissues and organs. But whether donation is a positive experience or a negative one—or whether families consider it at all—depends largely on your attitude and helpfulness. Do you facilitate donation or do you discourage it? Do you make it seem like a hurdle or a privilege?

I recently interviewed Raelynn Maloney, Family Support Coordinator for the Iowa Donor Network for more information on organ donation. She pointed out that the demand for organs far outweighs the number available for transplantation and thousands die each year while waiting for a second chance at life. As the national waiting list continues to grow, the number of organ donors has remained relatively unchanged over the past several years. Every 16 minutes a new name is added to the national waiting list, which today consists of more than 67,000 people. In 1998 the 5,799 organ donors in the United States provided transplants for only a small portion of these waiting patients.

Given the current donation rates, less than half of those waiting will ever be transplanted. according to the United Network for Organ Sharing (UNOS). While a national list does not exist for those waiting for tissue grafts and corneal transplants, there is a great need for donations of both tissues and eyes. Each year donors provide tissue for approximately 250,000 tissue grafting procedures, including hip replacements, heart valve transplants and ligament repairs. Last year more than 46,000 cornea transplants were also performed in the United States.

Generally, the option of donation is provided to families as they begin to make end-of-life decisions for their loved one. Though the procedures for offering this option differ significantly across the country, all potential donor families are provided with information necessary to make an informed decision about donation. The conversation about the donation process will likely include discussion about which organs and tissues can be donated, how long the process will take, where the procedure will take place, and what recipient information can be disclosed to them. Commonly held misconceptions about religion, cost and organ allocation procedures may also be clarified. In situations where brain death has occurred, the family is provided with a simple yet comprehensive explanation of brain death declaration and pronouncement prior to the donation discussion.

Once a family has decided to proceed with organ donation, the process may take between 10-30 hours. When organs will be recovered for transplant, the procurement agency spends much of this time working in the Critical Care Unit to determine which organs can be transplanted, locate recipients for each organ and coordinate the physician teams who will be recovering the organs.

The evaluation and recovery time for tissue and eye donations occurs more quickly than with organ donation. Time will be spent obtaining a thorough donor medical-social history and coordinating a recovery team. The length of the process is often dependent upon which tissues are being donated and the availability of a recovery room.

Often the donation conversation will generate questions that should be addressed prior to a family making a final decision regarding donation. The following are a few of the questions that may be asked and the answers that appropriately address each concern:

- *How long do we have to decide?*

  Reassure the family that they will not be rushed into a decision. However, they should be made aware of time constraints that might prevent them from donating certain organs or tissues if too much time elapses.

- *Where does the donation or recovery of the organs/tissues take place?*

  The recovery of organs and tissue is a surgical procedure and takes place in a hospital operating room. Care and respect for the person donating is given throughout the entire procedure.

- *Will my family member look different following the donation?*

  Because the recovery of organs and tissue is a surgical procedure, an incision will be made. However, this should not preclude your family from having an open casket funeral. If you should decide donation is right for you, you will want to consider what clothing would be best for an open casket viewing.

- *Will my family receive a bill for the donation?*

  A donor family should not be billed for anything related to the donation process. The costs are typically covered by the procurement agency involved in the donation, not by the family. There are occasions where the family is inadvertently sent a bill that includes charges incurred during the donation. Should this occur, families are encouraged to contact the procurement agency so the mistake can be remedied immediately.

Families of potential organ and tissue donors typically experience the sudden, often traumatic, death of someone loved. For all families the death is senseless. Some families must also cope with the knowledge that death resulted from the violent act of another or a self-inflicted wound.

The unique circumstances surrounding the catastrophic injury that led to brain death creates special needs for these families. Given no time to prepare and often little experience coping with such devastating news, donor families are in need of immediate and ongoing support.

Acknowledging the reality of the death is often complicated by the very nature of the death— brain death. A previously healthy person now lies motionless in a hospital bed with vital signs, yet a family is asked to comprehend and accept the irreversible nature of the injury and finality of the situation. A family may desire time with the body and reassurance that all medical treatment options have been exhausted.

Donor families often find comfort knowing they were able to help another live through their decision to donate. Over time they may develop a curiosity about those who received their family member's organs and tissues. Beyond this curiosity, donor families may experience feelings such as fear, anger, and sadness directly related to the decision to donate. They may fear the transplant will be unsuccessful, feel anger toward a recipient who fails to express gratitude for this gift, or grieve once again when a recipient dies. Ongoing support is critical to help meet the unique needs of donor families.

Funeral directors have a unique opportunity to provide support, reassurance and guidance to families who choose donation. One might assume the donation process ends once a family has signed the consent forms and leaves the hospital. However, the decision to donate can have a place in the funeral planning process. The following are just a few thoughts on how your staff can convey genuine support to donor families you serve:

- Regardless of your personal views on donation, honor and support every family's decision. A family should never be made to feel that their decision to donate has created a burden for the funeral home.

- Be prepared to answer questions. You are in a position to provide them with additional information about clothing the body to hide the surgical incision(s) made during the recovery process and preparing them for the initial viewing. Keep in mind that when brain death occurs and families choose organ donation, the last moments spent with their loved one were probably in the Intensive Care Unit. The body was still flush, warm and the heart still beating. These families in particular may need you to help them understand the transformation in appearance they will see.

• It may be important for some families to share with others during this time that their family member was a donor. Help them find ways to incorporate and share the decision to give a precious gift to others. For example, they may want to include this information in the obituary, on the program or incorporate it into the eulogy.

• Become familiar with the support services offered by your local organ procurement agencies. Collaboration will undoubtedly result in the best overall care of these families.

There are a number of outlets for obtaining information about organ, tissue and eye donation. I would encourage readers to contact their local organ or tissue procurement agency to obtain information specific to their area. The United Network for Organ Sharing (UNOS) website (www.unos.com) can also provide a plethora of information regarding national statistics, legislation, and policy on donation. For information specifically pertaining to tissue and eye donation, the American Association of Tissue Banks and the Eye Bank Association of America would be useful resources. Additionally, the National Kidney Foundation Donor Family Council has a variety of resources specifically for donor families at (800) 622-9010 or www.kidney.org.

For many bereaved families, the decision to donate organs is a helpful way to give meaning to a senseless loss. The beneficial impact of organ donation on the grief of most donor families is well documented. Family members have told me on many occasions that "perhaps the most positive aspect of my painful grief experience has been knowing that some other family has been brought comfort because of my loved one's gift." While recognizing this comfort, we would be well served to remember that it is always bittersweet comfort, and does not eradicate the pain of the grief that results from the death.

As funeral home staffs, you can make a critical difference in the lives of the bereaved families you are privileged to serve. I hope this information will assist you in making an empathetic connection with donor families you come in contact with.

For additional information on this important topic, you can contact Raelynn Maloney, Iowa Donor Network, 2732 Northgate Drive, Iowa City, Iowa 52245, (319) 337-7515.

Don'ts

In my work with funeral homes throughout North America, I have, on occasion, observed some of the following ways in which funeral homes create negative cues, which in turn alienate families. I call them the Dirty Dozen of customer service.

1. *The funeral home takes its customer base for granted*: "No matter what we do, we usually serve around 300 families a year."

2. *The funeral home has a merchandise-driven, as opposed to a customer-driven, philosophy.* More emphasis is placed on "the amount of the sale" than the quality of service provided.

3. *Employees assume the family doesn't want or need service.* For example, a family chooses a direct cremation with a church-based memorial service. One of the family members inquires about the funeral home having staff present at the service and are told, "No, you took service option #4; you don't really need us there." (A family member shared this recent example with me.)

4. *The funeral home or one or more of its employees has an attitude that projects,* "You can't please every family you serve, so why try?"

5. *The funeral home values pre-need service over at-need service.* This philosophy sometimes results in a subtle degradation of excellence in customer service levels to at-need families. The thinking is, "Well, we are guaranteeing our future with all the pre-need we are focusing on."

6. *Employees don't know how to provide excellent customer service.* The ability to perform at high service levels may be taken for granted. The fact that someone graduated from mortuary school or has worked in funeral service for years does not insure he or she has the knowledge, skills and personality to deliver excellent service.

7. *The funeral home doesn't have time to serve.* Focus on the "bottom-line" has resulted in some funeral homes being understaffed. It's difficult to deliver excellent service when you were awakened to do removals during the night,

made funeral arrangements for three families in the day and worked visitation that evening.

8. *Employees perceive "calls" as more of a pain to the business than a gain.* The customer is viewed as an interruption as opposed to an opportunity to serve and help.

9. *A transaction mentality has infiltrated the funeral home.* The focus is on, "How many have we had this month?" In other words, quantity of services provided takes precedence over quality of services provided.

10. *Staff turnover seems constant.* Consistency in personnel who work in coordination with others results in high quality service. If you are constantly training new staff, you are never functioning at peak service performance.

11. *The funeral home's customer service philosophy is, "If it ain't broke, don't fix it."* Employees, therefore, become discouraged from contributing ways to enhance family experiences.

12. *There is a perceived lack of challenge in providing excellent service.* This philosophy can be heard in comments like, "Well, we are the only ones in town who really know how to provide good service. We always have and we always will." This arrogance can lead to complacency. This attitude also sets in for those who perceive they have no competition for services.

At bottom, if you have no desire to serve bereaved families, get out of funeral service. If, on the other hand, you have a passion to serve families to the best of your ability, work to inspire everyone in the funeral home to measure every action against the needs and expectations of families served and strive to constantly exceed those expectations.

E's

Have you ever noticed how we North Americans often think that easier is better? It's easier to e-mail someone than to talk face to face. It's easier to grab a fast bite at McDonald's than to sit down and enjoy a real meal. It's easier to NOT volunteer at your child's school, to NOT get involved in your community, to NOT invite your neighbors over for dinner.

Easier and *more efficient* go hand in hand; they both seek value in less work and greater speed. But if you look in your heart of hearts, you will see that easier and more efficient are often much less effective.

I recently counseled a family that shared an experience with me that both saddened me and alerted me to the reality that some funeral homes (hopefully not many) may be confusing efficiency with effectiveness. As their funeral was being dismissed out of the chapel area and they were saying their final goodbyes to someone they loved deeply, the funeral home staff began wheeling in the casketed body for the next service. Naturally, the family was shocked by this action. Yes, maybe it was more efficient for the staff to begin setting up for the next funeral. It was also, rude, insensitive and inappropriate.

So, it occurred to me, perhaps every funeral home would be well-served to take pause and inventory any possibility that you are confusing ease and efficiency with effectiveness and the creation of meaningful funeral Experiences. I suggest you call a staff-meeting within the next week and review the following examples. What follows is only a sampling of the easier and more efficient decisions that get made every day at funeral homes. Perhaps you can add to the list from your observations.

Here's a tip: To uncover these examples in your funeral home, listen for your staff's use of the word "easier" in their conversations with families. Check off any of the examples below that might in some way apply to your funeral home and discuss the necessary actions to make changes immediately.

- You have someone on staff who is proud of how fast he can complete an arrangement conference. Worse yet, you have a reward system in place that reinforces quantity of families seen over the quality of the service arrangements provided.

- You have someone on your staff who encourages families to have visitation only one hour prior to services because it is "easier" for those attending. Worse yet, you have someone on staff that discourages visitations altogether.

- Your scheduling of services is more for your convenience than for the desires of the family. For example, the family would really like to have an afternoon service, but you encourage them to have a morning service in case you receive another call soon. Or your "rolling stock autos" are already committed to another service at the time the family prefers, but you don't want to rent so you encourage the family to hold the service at a time that is more convenient for you.

- You are not being compensated for a visitation with body present, so you decide not to offer the family any private time with the body.

- The family you are serving wanted to bring in the deceased person's favorite chair and place it by the casket during the visitation. You tell them, "No, that just wouldn't be convenient. We have never done that before."

- You have a practice of encouraging families to end the service in your chapel and not proceed to a committal, scattering, etc. After all, it's more convenient for you—but much less of an Experience for them!

- You discourage processions, explaining that it is just "easier" to meet at the cemetery. (One negative trend I am seeing is the dropping of the procession from the funeral home to the church in traditional Catholic mass funerals. Now, many "simply" meet at the church, thereby eliminating one more element of ceremony.)

- You get focused only on the commodity, i.e. "What did you sell?" versus the Experience, i.e. "What kind of service did you create?"

- You subtly or directly discourage flowers because you don't want to handle them.

- There is a death on Thursday with an arrangement conference on Friday. Visitation is set for Sunday with the service on Monday. The family asks if they can spend some time with the body on Saturday and a staff member decides no, it is more efficient to have the family come in for a private viewing prior to the public visitation on Sunday.

• A family member flies in from out of town and wants to see his father's body. The body is already casketed and a staff member is at the funeral home. The son is told, "No, it will easier if you just come in tomorrow afternoon as scheduled."

Easier and more efficient are most often not better. In funeral planning, easier and more efficient mean skipping steps and details that enrich the funeral Experience and help families heal.

As you work with the next family who comes through your door, shun the two bad E-words—Ease and Efficiency—and embrace the two good E-words—Effectiveness and Experience. Do this and you will have taken an important customer service step in the right direction.

Education

As we've said, today's families are often not aware of the value of funerals. They are not accustomed to making funeral arrangements and haven't attended many services. They have fewer ties to tradition. When a death occurs, many tend to think in terms of a "celebration of life," not a traditional funeral.

What if, when a potential new customer walked in your door, part of her experience of your funeral home included learning about the importance of funerals as well as the common elements of funerals? What if, in other words, your funeral home made the "educational realm" of the Experience a priority?

Several years ago I introduced an innovative program called "Honoring Family Choices" in conjunction with Batesville Management Services.

Honoring Family Choices is a set of signage and literature that inform, educate and offer customers choices about all the elements of the funeral ceremony. Through visual support such as signage, photos and literature, the purposes of various elements of ceremony—visitation, symbols, music, committal, gathering, etc.—are concisely defined, thus teaching all who visit your funeral home (including both at-need and pre-need families) about the *value* of the elements of ceremony.

Another way to educate families about the value of funerals is through community workshops (see Workshops) and delivering presentations for community groups (see Speeches).

Think of yourself as a funeral service ambassador. If it were your job to save funeral service from going the way of the mastodon (and it is your job, if you think about it), how would you help re-educate people about the value of funerals? Creating exceptional Experiences is the best way, of course; walk the talk and word will soon spread that you're doing something amazing. But enthusiastically educating your community about funerals—what's involved in a funeral, why we have them, what the possibilities are—is also critical. Talk the talk, too.

E-mail

The day is coming when you'll receive just as much e-mail from families (if not more) than phone calls. Are you gearing up for that day?

Some families will contact you via e-mail because it's more comfortable for them; after all, talking to a funeral director face-to-face is a grim prospect for some folks :) E-mail is also a quick method of relaying information around-the-clock. Let's say you want to confirm an arrangement conference at noon tomorrow and it's 10:00 at night. Well, it's too late to call the family but it's never too late to e-mail them. E-mail is also a great way to send information to a group of people all at once. Some families may want you to e-mail dates and times or contact information to friends and relatives across the country (or across the globe!).

The same rules that apply to telephone contact apply to e-mail. Respond promptly and courteously. Reply clearly and in detail. Use positive language. Be sure to include all your contact information at the bottom of each e-mail: your name, funeral home name, address, phone and fax numbers, etc.

Also learn to use all the e-mail tools at your disposal. You can send and receive photos and text and graphics files via e-mail. You can send maps to family members and obituaries to newspapers. You can even send and receive music.

Boomers and especially X- and Y-geners are e-mailers. You need to be, too.

Empathy

One of the foundations of excellent customer service is communication. To be helpful to the families you serve, you must communicate with them effectively and make them feel cared for.

We all have probably observed some funeral directors whom we would call "natural helpers." Actually, the helping skills that seem so natural to them are more likely characteristics and qualities they have learned and developed over time. The most important quality is empathy, but there are others described below, as well. You, too, have the capacity to learn and make use of these helping qualities.

Empathy

Empathy is the ability to perceive another's experience and then—this is the key—communicate that perception back to the person. As a helping funeral director, I listen to you , and though I cannot experience your experience, I begin to have a mental picture of the essence of what you are describing.

Perhaps the most vital part of this characteristic is the ability to convey accurate empathy. Empathetic responsiveness requires the ability to go beyond factual detail and to become involved in the other person's feeling world, but always with the "as if" quality of taking another's role without personally experiencing what the other person experiences. If you actually experienced the same emotions as the person you are trying to help, you would be overinvolved. To have empathy for another person does not constitute the direct expression of one's own feelings, but rather focuses exclusively on the feelings expressed by another, thereby conveying an understanding of them.

You know that empathy has been communicated when the family member feels the funeral home staff "understands." As you know, to say simply "I understand how you feel" is not enough. The response goes beyond the "I understand how you feel" level to the "You really are feeling a sense of loss" level. In other words, empathy is communicated both verbally and nonverbally by understanding the person at the emotional level.

Respect

Respect is the helpful funeral director's ability to communicate his or her belief that everyone has the inherent capacity and right to choose and make decisions. Respect requires a nonpossessive caring for and affirmation of another person, respecting another's right to be who and what they are. This quality involves a receptive attitude that embraces the other person's feelings, opinions and uniqueness—even those radically different from his or her own.

So, the dimension of respect is communicated when the family feels they have been allowed to make decisions without being pressured and when their opinions have been considered important. Remembering what the person has said, demonstrating sensitivity and courtesy, and showing respect for the person's feelings and beliefs are the essences of communicating respect.

Warmth and Caring

The warm and caring funeral director cultivates a sense of personal closeness, as opposed to professional distance, with the families he serves. Showing you are warm and caring is particularly helpful in the early phases of building a helping relationship. The dimension of warmth is communicated primarily nonverbally. For example, in the funeral home, touch is one of the most important nonverbal behaviors.

Warmth is a very powerful dimension in the helping process. In fact, when a discrepancy exists between verbal and nonverbal behavior, people almost always believe the nonverbal. A person's nonverbal behavior seldom lies. Consequently, a person who has excellent verbal communication skills, but lacks "warm" nonverbal behavior, would more than likely be perceived by the family as not helpful, indifferent, cold or uncaring.

Genuineness

Genuineness is the ability to present oneself sincerely. As a helping funeral director, this is your ability to be freely yourself—without phoniness, role playing or defensiveness. It's when your outer words and behaviors match your inner feelings.

The dimension of genuineness involves disclosing how you feel about an issue. One important caveat: Try not to tell others how you feel too early because your opinion may interfere with their ability to make a decision. Genuineness can be very helpful, but timing is important. The family's feelings should be explored first, followed by genuineness on the part of the funeral home staff. This is not to say that staff should be phony, but rather they should be non-judgmental. This attitude will help the family feel that the staff cares about them as individuals. You can earn the right to be genuine with others through first developing the relationship.

As your funeral home works to continuously improve its customer service, be sure you spend some time analyzing how you and your staff members can be more helpful to your customers. Empathy, respect, warmth and caring, and genuineness are all important components in that process.

Energy

Give thought to the energy you bring to your position at the funeral home. We all give off energy, be it positive or negative. The families you serve will be able to sense your individual energy. Moreover, as an important member of the funeral home team, your energy either contributes to the workteam's desire to serve or is a drag on the team. In other words, you are either helping or hurting the team you serve on. Are you conveying positive energy in the funeral home? Or are you bringing destructive energy tht detracts from your capacity to be a value-added team member?

Another way to think about this concept of positive versus negative energy would be as follows: A bereaved family chooses to use your funeral home. They come in for the arrangement conference and are left standing inside the entryway without being welcomed for 10 minutes. When they are greeted, the funeral director has a frown on his face, does not project an ounce of warmth and caring, isn't knowledgeable about creating meaningful funeral Experiences and has a general attitude of "Let's just get this over with." Obviously, the families you serve deserve better! Your energy and attitude are where customer service starts.

Eulogies

We know that the more personalized the funeral, the more meaningful it will be to those in attendance. One important way of making the funeral a fitting tribute to the person who died is through the eulogy.

Let's remind ourselves that eulogy is a transliteration of the Greek word that means "to bless" or "to praise." The eulogy, or period of remembrance, is for saying good things about, or "blessing," the person who is being remembered. It is a time to pay tribute to the person's life. The eulogy acknowledges the unique life of the person who died and affirms the significance of that life for all that shared in it.

I sometimes encounter clergy and others who believe that eulogies are somehow unnecessary, perhaps even bad. Some believe that eulogies takes the focus off God. I totally disagree. Remembering a life lived and being supported by faith are not mutually exclusive.

Understanding the need to embrace memories

One of the central needs of mourning involves allowing and encouraging oneself to have a relationship of memory. Helping people begin to shift from a relationship of presence to memory often begins with the funeral. The memories embraced during the funeral set the tone for the changed nature of the relationship.

A meaningful eulogy is a vital step in the process of getting this need met. Some people in our mourning-avoiding culture do not have an understanding of the role of memories in the grief experience. They tend to move people away from— instead of toward—their grief.

In my experience, remembering the past makes hoping for the future possible. As I often note, "You must listen to the music of the past to sing in the present and dance into the future." The future becomes open to new experiences only to the extent that those in grief embrace their past.

Distinguishing the obituary from the eulogy

It's also critically important to remember the distinction between an obituary and a eulogy. We have probably all been part of funerals where the officiant simply read the obituary but referred to it as a eulogy.

In contrast to the eulogy, the word obituary originates from the Latin word obit, which means departure. The obituary is usually a written declaration of a person's death. Facts outlined in the obituary usually include: the person's name; date and place of birth; date and place of death; place of employment; service club memberships; and names of survivors. As you know, some obituaries are more creative and interesting than others. However, simply reading the obituary is not a substitute for a meaningful eulogy or period of remembrance being integrated into the funeral service.

Some eulogy tips

Let's remind ourselves about some other important points surrounding eulogies:

- The eulogy may be delivered by a clergy person, a family member or a friend of the person who died. This person is called the "eulogist."

- Some non-faith families you serve may prefer to refer to this element of ceremony as "the period of remembrance." You should honor this request.

- Those who serve as eulogists are not always familiar with helpful guidelines in preparing a meaningful eulogy. Your funeral home would be well-served to make some helpful guidelines available to these people.

Instead of a traditional eulogy delivered by one person, several people can share memories during the eulogy time. Families often comment on how meaningful this has been to them. The families you serve today are teaching you that they want to be more involved than in the past. Historically (and unfortunately, sometimes today), the funeral was all too often a passive experience for those in attendance. As we listen to families, we find they often want the funeral to be as unique and personal as possible. A participant-oriented eulogy can help achieve this goal.

This form of eulogy may be done formally—by having three or four people speak in succession at the podium—or informally—by asking those attending the funeral to stand up and share memories spontaneously. Part of your role as a funeral director is to make this option known to those you have the privilege of serving. Yes, participant-oriented eulogies take more time. But remember—never confuse efficiency with effectiveness.

There is no right or wrong way to eulogize the person who died. If you help families to share memories and honor the person's life, you will have added more value to the funeral experience.

Excellence

If the goal of your funeral home is to help the families you serve create meaningful funeral Expriences and then some, you're living the pursuit of excellence. The *and then some* mantra is a philosophy and practice that says, "Our funeral home will take care of grieving families' needs . . . *and then some*. Our funeral home will work to anticipate the needs and wants of families served . . . *and then some*. Our funeral home will serve families not only in pre-need and at-need, but in post-need . . . *and then some*. It's through the *and then some* philosophy that you impact the profitability of your funeral home and the stability of your future.

Family

A funeral director friend and I were recently chatting at a convention. As he reflected on his life, he lamented, "I don't seem to have time for my wife, my kids, or myself lately. I get tired of calling home and apologizing: Sorry, I have to work late again. Sometimes I feel like a stranger in my own house."

Perhaps my friend's frustrations sound familiar to you. If you have been over-working and under-relating, I invite you to read on and explore the importance of balancing customer care with family care.

As you may well know, funeral service and work overload can easily go together. To note just a few stresses:

• a constantly fluctuating schedule

• competing demands for time and attention from work and family

• new challenges in funeral service that demand newly refined skills and absolute excellence in work performance

All too often funeral directors I visit with are devoting so much time and energy to the funeral home that they have nothing left for their spouses, their children, or even themselves. Actually, many suffer from time starvation related to their home life.

Commitment to your life partner and children has to be a priority and in funeral service there are many competitors for this critical time. Regardless how busy you are, you must nourish your couple time and parenting time. Healthy love cannot be taken for granted. Try to imagine, even momentarily, what your life would be like without your life partner and children.

Family time can be particularly hard hit by the time presures of funeral service. A review of studies on family stress reveals time pressures to be at the top of the list. One major study found that four of the top stresses have to do with lack of time:

• insufficient couple time

• insufficient "me" time

- insufficient family playtime
- overscheduled family calenders

Take pause for a moment and be startled by the time averages involving spouse and children. Spouse-to-spouse time averages as little as four minutes a day of meaningful conversation. Quality time between parent and child is in similar snippets: between thirty-seven seconds and five minutes a day, depending on the study. How do you compare? Is your life partner expressing concern that you don't have time to connect, to be present to each other? Have you lost the excitement and romance that brought you together? Are your children time-starved for your attention? Worse yet, do they seem indifferent to even wanting to spend time with you?

Family Time: Five Essentials

1. Schedule Family Time

Have you ever noticed how family members often meet coming and going? Slow down and schedule time together. One meal a day together should be a bare minimum. Plan a family night once a month where you focus on special interests the family can share.

2. Be Available and Listen

Ask yourself if you shift roles easily and appropriately from work to home, from earner to nurturing parent and partner. Ask open-ended questions, and listen and learn from your family members instead of making assumptions. Actually, listening unconditionally and demonstrating interest in your partner and children is the greatest tribute you can give them.

3. Give Time, Not Material Objects

Don't make the mistake of thinking you can buy the love of your family members. Remember that nothing can replace your presence, your hug, your companionship.

4. Keep Your Romance Alive

Look for opportunities to add romance to your partner or marriage relationship. Don't forget the importance of the occasional flowers (the ones you bring home from funerals don't count!), the unexpected love note, or the overnight getaway.

5. Model Respect for Each Other

Create a home environment where each family member respects the individual needs of all others. Emulate love, trust, compassion and caring. Above all, provide your children a solid foundation of principles and values.

First Impressions

It's been said that clothes don't make the man, but when it comes to the funeral Experience, first impressions definitely count.

A well-known reality in customer service is that first impressions are lasting impressions. They also serve as indications of things to come. A disheveled funeral director may cause families to doubt his or her general level of competence and ability to take care of them before, during and after the funeral.

Actually, everything about the funeral director and other staff members, including appearance, communicates something about the level of service the bereaved family can expect. Not just dress but body language, tone of voice, rate of speech and a variety of other "presentation" skills affect the service impressions people have of both individual staff members and the entire funeral home. These impressions give the message that "We are caring, competent, and here to help you," or, at the other extreme, "We are not sure we can take care of ourselves, let alone serve you during this difficult time in your life."

If you have a funeral director who isn't dressing the part, you may have to adopt strict dress codes and standards of personal hygiene. While you might like to think such formalities aren't necessary, some employees just don't get it. Your staff person may be among those who need very direct communication about the importance of appearance. You have given him the opportunity to respond to what was hopefully your supportive way of requesting his improvement in this area. You must now be even more direct and emphasize the need for immediate change. You might offer to help him improve his appearance, or better yet, refer him to a dress consultant through a local clothing store. If he still refuses to change, you may be forced to take more extreme measures.

Gatherings

Most funerals formally come to an end when the mourners gather to share a meal and talk about the person who died. This is an extremely important part of the funeral Experience because it is an informal time of release after the more formal elements of ceremony. It is a time for the "telling of the story" of the death—a healing and necessary ritual for the primary mourners. It encourages the sharing of memories and the supporting of one another. It also helps families begin to make the transition from death back to life again.

Does your funeral home have a nice reception area with kitchenette or facilities for caterers? If not, you're missing out on a wonderful opportunity to both generate revenues and help families.

If you do have a reception area, are you using it to best effect? Gatherings are perhaps the best time to display memerobilia and photos. Some families are using this time to share a memory video of the person who died.

Also important is ambiance. Personalized music, flowers, attractive lighting, comfortable seating around round tables (which are more conducive to conversation than rectangular tables), plants, upholstered chairs arranged in conversation groupings, large windows, architectural details such as molding and perhaps a gas fireplace all contribute to the Experience and can transform a cold reception area into one that makes people want to linger and enjoy each other's company.

Last but not least, the refreshments should be both tasty and attractive. What are you doing to help ensure this is so? Do you have a pre-screened list of good caterers? Do you supply serving tables, nice serving pieces, candles, ice? Remember—the funeral home that best serves today's families is an events coordinator, and events with blah food and blah surroundings are neither memorable nor worth the money.

Groundrules

NEVER SAY NO. You've heard the edict "the customer's always right." Unless it would be violating laws to do so, always handle the family's every request gracefully and eagerly. There is no such thing as a standard funeral for a typical family. Every family is unique; every funeral should be unique.

PARTNER WITH CLERGY. To be as helpful as you can in planning a meaningful ceremony, you must work as closely as possible with the clergy member who'll be officiating. This won't always be possible; some clergy will be resistant to your help or suggestions. But where possible, offer to help create a personalized ceremony.

BE GENUINE WITH THE FAMILY. Too often, funeral directors are seen as "behind-the-scenes," Lurch-like characters who embalm bodies, wear black suits and nod respectfully. This isn't a helpful demeanor! Instead, be compassionate. Be human. Think of how you act when you're helping neighbor Bob fix his fencepost—casual, direct, friendly, genuine.

BE SPIRITUAL. If you are a person of faith (and most people who work with the dying and the bereaved are), express your spirituality with the families you serve. It's inappropriate to impose your beliefs on a family with different ones, but often it's appropriate to tap into the family's belief system in personalizing the ceremony.

NO HOVERING. There's a difference between being genuinely helpful and responsive and hovering. Hovering is standing at the back of the room during the visitation. Being helpful is expressing warmth and empathy then leaving the family to mourn.

Helping

The helping relationship, which begins with your initial contact with the bereaved family, is so critical because it becomes the basis for meaningful contact between you and family members. (And people in crisis are typically open to the evolution of a helping relationship with persons who have the knowledge and ability to help them.) Through the context of the helping relationship, a climate is created in which people can explore their concerns and begin to make decisions about what will be helpful to them at this time. As the relationship grows, an opportunity exists to aid people in the process of self-exploration, self-understanding, and choices of action.

Phases in the helping relationship

A helping relationship can be visualized as having phases that demarcate its stages from beginning to end. The seven phases outlined below are typical of funeral director-customer relationships, but they do not always occur in this specific sequence, nor are all phases always present. The way in which bereaved family members approach the helping relationship often helps determine the sequence and length of the phases. For example, some family members come with very specific requests, such as direct disposition of the body. Others wonder what their funeral alternatives are. Obviously, these two examples demand a different kind of helping process. The diverse needs and desires of different families, therefore, call for some variation in these phases.

PHASE 1. *Entering Into the Helping Relationship*

A member of the family (or hospital staff, hospice staff, nursing home staff, etc.) has phoned your funeral home and informed you of the death of a family member. The family has asked for your assistance.

PHASE 2. *Building a Helping Relationship*

You respond by showing a willingness to assist the family. You offer counsel on what needs to be done now. You respond with concern and care to any questions they might have.

PHASE 3. Helping the Family Understand Their Alternatives

You listen and explore with the family the variety of alternatives available to them with regard to the funeral. You gather facts, explore feelings, and seek mutual understanding.

PHASE 4. Consolidation and Planning

You assist the family in coming to decisions about the funeral that best meets their needs. You jointly develop a specific action plan designed to best meet their emotional and spiritual needs at this time.

PHASE 5. Implementation and Action

You conduct a funeral service that follows the planning model developed with the family. You bring together a variety of helping resources within your community to assist in this action-oriented helping process.

PHASE 6. Conclusion of the Funeral Process

You assist the family with a sense of closure upon completion of the funeral. You might join in the fellowship that often occurs following the completion of the funeral.

PHASE 7. Aftercare or Post-Funeral Service Follow-Up

After the funeral, you might have a structured follow-up program to offer additional assistance to families. You may serve as an information and referral source for additional help-oriented services within your community.

Funeral directors who can warmly and effectively guide their customers through these seven phases will have truly met their customers' needs. And that, after all, is what excellence in customer service is all about.

Hiring

Working competently in a funeral home usually requires a multitude of skills. Creating exceptional funeral Experiences for today's families as well as pleasing interactions with the general public takes many skills as well as genuine caring.

A funeral director who consistently delivers great customer service is part counselor, part teacher, part advocate, part technician, part host, part ambassador and even part accountant. This is not an easy job description to fill and many people are not naturally suited for it.

Screening for personalities that match funeral service

Most managers and owners who hire funeral directors tend to look at education, technical skills and work experience. Not that these qualifications aren't important, but more often than not, it's the values and personality of the funeral director that will influence job success or failure.

In my experience, empathy and caring are among the most important personality characteristics to select into potential funeral home employees. You can teach people to say "Good evening" and "How may I help you?", but you can't train people to care. They need to bring it with them to the funeral home.

After all, people who only pretend to care will reveal themselves at some point. You can't fake caring for very long. The more stressful times get (funeral homes are a natural breeding ground for high stress), the more quickly the lack of genuine caring reveals itself.

Defining personality

Personality consists of three important elements: values, beliefs, and behavioral preferences. Let's take a brief look at each of these elements.

Values:

What a person values influences their behavior. Some people value technical skills, like embalming, more than others. Some poeple value the process of planning and preparing for the funeral more than others. Some people value the importance of providing aftercare services to families more than others.

We all value different things. Our values play a major role in molding our overall personalities. As managers and owners interview a potential new hire, probing questions must be asked that clarify values. If there is a mismatch of values with your funeral home's needs, now is the time to determine it—not ten years later, when you decide to let somene go because they never had the same values your funeral home aspires to uphold.

Beliefs:

What a person believes at their core drives their actions. At the most basic level, what does the funeral director believe about the importance of ceremony at times of death? Does he or she understand why we have funerals and how they help people create conditions to mourn well? Or, on the other hand, does the potential hire believe that funeral service is a profession where you can wear a suit, drive really nice cars and make lots of money? Reasons why one selects funeral service as a profession are critically important to explore in the interview process.

Behavioral Preferences:

Some funeral directors want to interact with families and the public all of the time. Others would be happy to be behind the scenes doing body preparation all the time. Both needs are important, but what are the needs of your funeral home? How does the potential hire match up with those needs? In most funeral homes, you need people who are willing to do both—interact well with the public and work well behind the scenes. Some funeral directors want managers who provide a lot of structure and rules to guide behavior, while others want to be left alone and require less supervision. Again, how will the potential employee fit into your unique funeral home?

Without a doubt, the quality of service your funeral home provides will be dependent upon the quality of funeral directors and support staff you hire. Excellent funeral directors have a "service personality" and genuinely care about the families they serve. As you work to hire exceptional employees, spend time getting to know an applicant's personality and consider if he or she best meets the needs of your funeral home.

Qualities to look for

Yet another way to consider whom to hire is to review the following list of qualities. If during the course of your interviews you meet potential employees with these qualities, consider yourself lucky.

1. **A history of "service orientation."** Your goal is to consciously "select-in" those people with a predisposed customer service orientation and "select-out" those deficient in this area. During the interview, try to determine if potential employees have demonstrated, in both their life and work experience, that they like people and that they like serving them. Many may tell you that they like people, but look closely at their previous experiences to see if they "walk the talk."

Specific characteristics that often go hand-in-hand with a strong service orientation include the following:

- *sensitivity and warmth toward others* —You should feel this in your interview. If you don't, "select-out."

- *flexibility*—Be certain to design some specific questions that explore this critical area. You might ask, for example, how the interviewee would feel about working late or coming in early to help a bereaved family.

- *enthusiasm*—Try to determine if the applicant has a genuine interest in funeral service or is just after a paycheck.

2. **A "teachable" attitude.** People who don't feel they already know it all but instead welcome new ideas make good team players. While your potential employees should be confident in both their technical and interpersonal abilities, watch out for rigidity. Again, design some interview questions that will help you determine if applicants are open to learning new things.

3. **A team player.** Obviously, funeral service requires a team of people working together to best meet the needs of bereaved families. Ask yourself if an applicant would fit in with the current team. I recently visited a funeral home where one employee's humorlessness made him a misfit. He ostracized himself from the other employees (who all had healthy senses of humor) and communicated with them only when absolutely necessary. I suspect that his "way of being" also put off the bereaved families he worked with.

4. **A problem-solving mentality.** While "team-fit" is critical, it is also important to hire people who have sufficient problem-solving skills to make some decisions on their own. Employees who can solve problems autonomously and quickly will be better prepared to serve your customers. Let's say a bereaved family has a special request for their loved one's funeral. Would your new employee say, "No, we don't do that"? Or keeping the family's best interest in mind, would he or she instead reply, "Yes, I think we can arrange that for you. Let me look into how your request can most appropriately be handled."

✓5. **A pleasing appearance.** While your employees certainly don't need to be supermodels, they should dress and carry themselves in a way that inspires confidence in your customers. As the saying goes, first impressions are lasting ones, and poor grooming or odd mannerisms can cause bereaved families to doubt the competence of an employee and thus the competence of your funeral home.

The Art of the Interview

I find that while employers are often aware of the above qualities, they don't often create interviews that best highlight them. I suggest that funeral homes develop what is called a "structural interview"—one that uses open-ended questions to focus on *specific behavioral characteristics* important to the position they are trying to fill.

Suppose, for example, you are hiring a manager for a new branch location. The manager's major responsibilities will be to hire, train and supervise an entirely new staff. Critical job-related behavioral characteristics, then, will be *people development* and *leadership*. Here are a few sample questions that would allow you to asses an applicant's skills in these two areas:

1. How would you identify people who would make excellent arrangement conference counselors? Please specify your criteria.

2. What kind of training/orientation program would you set up? How would you implement such a program?

3. What kind of appraisal review process would you set up with the employees? What expectations would you have related to your own appraisal review?'

4. How would you respond to an employee who does things counter to your training and supervision?

5. What is your perception of what motivates employees to stay focused on excellence in customer service?

Other job-related behavioral characteristics for a successful location manager might include: planning and organizational skills, verbal communication skills, and delegation skills. Specific interview questions can be developed that would inform you about the person's skill levels in these areas.

If you want to reduce your failure rate in hiring employees, work to develop structural interviews that explore specific behavioral characteristics.

Seek Out Excellent Employees

With the current shortage of well-qualified funeral service employees, you may be well-served to recruit already-employed people. Don't just wait for resumes to come across your desk—actively seek out the star performers in funeral service. They are often flattered when contacted and may be willing to make a move for the right opportunity. Hiring the best employees will no doubt save you both time and money. Actually, exceptional employees will make you money in the long run.

Holidays

Chestnuts roasting on an open fire. Jingle bells. Joy to the world!

For people in grief, especially the newly bereaved, the winter holidays are nothing to sing about. Yet everywhere, all around them—their shopping centers, their TV programs, their neighborhoods, their places of worship—the world is abuzz with the joyful frenzy of Thanksgiving, Christmas, Hanukkah and Kwanza.

This dissonance between what's going on outside and what the bereaved are feeling inside makes the holidays particularly painful. Then there are the memories of all those holidays past, when the person who died was so much alive and so much a part of their celebrations. Such bittersweet memories can be particularly hard to embrace in the midst of all the holiday cheer.

And let's not forget the bereaved family's difficulties in deciding how to celebrate this year. Do they carry on with longstanding traditions, even if they're not in the mood? Who will cook and wrap presents and organize get-togethers when nobody even feels like getting out of bed in the morning?

These wounded, mourning families need your help this holiday season. As death and grief care experts in your community, you have a unique opportunity to reach out to them, to enhance the experience you provide to families served. Your staff not only knows these families, they have been a part of each unique family's experience with loss. Who better to step up to the plate and say, "I understand that your loss makes the holidays very hard for you. We'd like to help."?

The Holiday Remembrance Program

As part of their aftercare efforts, many funeral homes across the country are stepping up to the plate this season. Hundreds will be hosting Holiday Remembrance Programs in their communities this November or December.

What exactly is a Holiday Remembrance Program? Well, everybody does it a little differently, but the general idea is to invite bereaved families to attend a presentation and/or ceremony that acknowledges their loss, remembers the people who died and gives them a safe place to embrace their holiday grief.

Recently I talked to bereavement coordinators at four funeral homes with a combined total of 25 years' experience planning and holding Holiday Remembrance Ceremonies. They are: Myrna Gordon of Alden-Waggoner Funeral Home in Boise, Idaho; Sr. Diane Liona of Chapey Funeral Home in Islip, New York; Jennifer Mirabella of Horan & McConaty Funeral Home in Denver, Colorado; and Robin Miller of Thompson-Miller Funeral Home in Butler, Pennsylvania. I would like to share their wealth of ideas and knowledge with you in the hopes that your funeral home, too, will consider helping bereaved families this holiday season.

Program Format

Will your program consist of grief education or holiday ceremony? Three of the four funeral homes I spoke with combine the two.

Chapey Funeral Home, for example, holds a two-hour, formal luncheon in the late afternoon. Sister Liona gives a presentation on how to deal with grief during the holidays followed by a candlelight memorial service led by the funeral directors. Centerpieces at each table contain four candles (standing for memories, grief, etc.) and each guest has a vigil candle of their own to hold. Following the short ceremony, guests, who have been grouped at round tables according to type of loss, often stay to chat with each other for a half hour or so.

Horan & McConaty's program format is similar. At their one-hour evening program entitled "A Time of Remembrance," Jennifer Mirabella first gives a talk on practical ways to handle holiday grief and to memorialize the person who died during the holidays. Mirabella, director of bereavement support but also a deaconal minister in the Lutheran church, then leads a short memorial candlelighting service. Guests are given slips of paper on which to write the names of the people they are there to remember; during the service, funeral home staff read the names aloud.

At Thompson-Miller's "Tinsel and Tears" annual program, held in the evening and lasting about two hours, Robin Miller and her staff offer guests suggestions for handling holiday grief, dealing with children during the holidays and planning for this year's holidays. Miller also reads Bruce Conley's "Griever's Holiday Bill of Rights" and several short excerpts from the *Chicken Soup for the Soul* books. The program concludes with a holiday memorial candle-lighting ceremony.

Alden-Waggoner's holiday program does not include grief education per se, but is rather a non-denominational church service. Held in the funeral home chapel, the program is advertised as a "Service of Remembrance" and is led by a minister. The service includes a message by the minister and "lots of uplifting Christmas music," says Myrna Gordon. As with the other three programs, this one also ends with a candlelighting ceremony. Names of the people who have died (submitted by guests) are also read aloud by the minister.

Who Attends

The majority of the funeral homes I talked to invite not only families served to their holiday program, but everyone in the community. The funeral home's entire staff is also encouraged to attend, creating a special opportunity for funeral directors and support staff to reconnect to families they have worked with. "When families walk in, they see and talk to the staff members who helped them with their funeral and they feel like they haven't been forgotten," says Sister Liona. "Sometimes they get a little overwhelmed, in a good way, that the funeral home hasn't forgotten about them."

Alden-Waggoner's service is open to families served as well as the whole community. Last year, for their 6th annual service, 175 people attended. "It's about half and half families we've served and families we haven't," explains Gordon. "The first year we had no idea what to expect and we overplanned. We had 25 people come and we were so disappointed. But then those people who came told us how much it meant to them. Since then, it's grown every single single year. Many families make it part of their holiday tradition and return year after year."

Thompson-Miller's program is also open to the community. Drawing from a community of 25,000, they have about 50-70 people attend every year. Neither Alden-Waggoner or Thompson-Miller request RSVPs.

A five-location funeral home in Denver, Horan & McConaty hosts their holiday program at each location on a different night of the week. Families served as well as the community at large are invited, and an average of 100 people attend each program. Mirabella does ask for RSVPs so she can plan for refreshments and candles.

"We've been doing this program for about 10 years," says Mirabella. "What's been really nice is that people will call and ask, 'Are you going to do that service again?' Our aftercare program is here for anyone in the community—not just our customers—and this program is part of that."

And finally, only families served during the last calendar year are invited to Chapey Funeral Home's more formal luncheon. Their two locations do a total of 600-700 funerals per year; about 200 people attend the holiday program each year. RSVPs are required, though Liona always reserves an extra table or two for drop-ins or last-minute sign-ups.

Giving mourners a chance to talk to each other is one of the most significant benefits of holiday remembrance programs. "It gives people a chance to be with others whose hearts feel similarly," says Mirabella. Gordon agrees: "We want to give people a place where they can come and feel safe and remember their loved one as well as get something in return—a feeling of hope and an opportunity to interact with others who have had a loss. It's hard to talk to someone who hasn't been there about your grief."

Getting the Word Out

So how do you let bereaved families know about your upcoming program? The funeral homes I visited with use invitations, advertising or a combination of both.

Using their in-house mailing lists, Alden-Waggoner, Horan & McConaty and Chapey Funeral Homes mail invitations. Horan & McConaty adds value by having individual funeral directors send invitations to the families they have served and by tucking a copy of a brochure I authored entitled "Helping Yourself Heal During the Holiday Season" (available from Batesville Management Services) in the invitation.

All but Chapey Funeral Home also advertise their programs in their area newspapers. Alden-Waggoner even advertises their Service of Remembrance on local radio and TV. Talk about a great opportunity to advertise your funeral home as a supporter of your community!

Scheduling Considerations

When should you hold a holiday remembrance program? Anywhere from mid-November to mid-December, according to my gracious information-sharers.

Thompson-Miller plans theirs for 7-9 pm one evening in mid-November because, says Miller, they want to help families prepare for Thanksgiving as well as the December holidays. Chapey's holiday luncheon is also held in mid-November, from 3-5 in the afternoon. Horan & McConaty opt for early December. "Not too close to Christmas but after Thanksgiving," says Mirabella. Their program is shorter—about an hour long—and takes place in the evening at 7 pm. Alden-Waggoner's memorial service is held on a Saturday night about two weeks before Christmas and lasts about 40 minutes, followed by refreshments and visiting time. Why Saturday night? Because their funeral home is not normally open then, so the service doesn't conflict with visitations and funerals.

Sites and Seating

You can choose to hold your holiday remembrance program at your funeral home or off-site at a local meeting room or restaurant. The former may depend on your facilities. Does your funeral home have a chapel or visitation room spacious enough to hold 50-200 people? Will people feel comfortable there? Do you have kitchen facilities for preparing and serving refreshments?

Both Horan & McConaty and Alden-Waggoner hold their holiday programs on-site. Chapey rents out a reception hall at a restaurant in town. And Thompson-Miller holds their program at the local YWCA in a nice meeting room.

Refreshments and Other Niceties

The importance of atmosphere was mentioned by all of the funeral homes. Horan & McConaty sets out small Norfolk Island pines ablaze in white lights. Alden-Waggoner lavishly decorates their chapel with a huge Christmas tree and lots and lots of candles. Chapey's luncheon includes formal table settings with china, linens and exquisite floral centerpieces. "People walk in feeling very nurtured and cared for," says Liona. "It's very elegant."

Alden-Waggoner and Horan & McConaty also give out Christmas decorations to guests. "Each year we have a different ornament," says Gordon, "so the minister weaves the meaning of that year's ornament into his message."

Informational packets are also made available to guests at the holiday programs.

And what about holiday music? Chapey Funeral Home hires a pianist to play soft background music during the ceremony. Horan & McConaty play taped, generic instrumental music in the background. And Alden-Waggoner hires local musicians (this year it will be an all-women's singing group) to perform "uplifting" Christmas music.

I probably don't have to remind you funeral directors about one final nicety, but I will anyway, just in case: Don't forget to put out boxes of tissues!

Budget

The four funeral homes I talked with hadn't drawn up in advance or tracked formal budgets for their holiday remembrance programs. But how much you'll spend is largely dependent on three things: 1) publicity (including invitations); 2) ceremony or program extras; and 3) refreshments.

Obviously, printing and mailing hundreds of invitations can be costly, but it's a non-threatening, compassionate way for you to reconnect with past customers. Any advertising you do is also money well-spent on your funeral home's image and visibility in your community.

The ceremony itself needn't be expensive, although you may need to pay small honorariums for speakers or musicians. When you're calculating your budget, don't forget to include the cost of handouts, programs and favors.

Refreshments for your holiday program can be as simple—and as inexpensive—as cookies and punch. More elaborate fare might be a memorable touch, but don't forget that a full stomach isn't the main thing you want guests to leave with. Instead, it's the feeling that they've been remembered and given the opportunity to mourn their loss during the holidays.

All four holiday programs are free. In the past, Thompson-Miller has put out donation baskets to help offset the cost of refreshments, but found this to be unsuccessful. This year they're considering charging guests a nominal fee.

One Final Pitch

Obviously I believe that holiday remembrance programs can be extremely healing for mourners. But I also believe that being seen as a compassionate funeral home that genuinely cares about the families it serves long after they've paid their bills is just plain good business.

Though Jennifer Mirabella of Horan & McConaty emphasizes that they don't hold their holiday programs for public relations reasons, she says that John Horan, one of the owners, implicitly understands their PR value. "It affirms relationships we've already developed *and* it creates new ones," she says. "I really think the work we do is about honoring relationships . . . and that doesn't end."

Innovation

Innovate or evaporate. Those are pretty much your two choices in funeral service today.

Wilson & Kratzer Chapel of San Ramon Valley, Danville, California, has chosen to innovate. This 3-year-old funeral home is having great success offering innovative and personalized funeral experiences for families. While you may think your community's needs are more traditional, and that what goes on in a California funeral home has nothing to do with you, I suggest you think again. Consider how rapidly trends can move from one area of North America to another.

Wilson & Kratzer Chapel is part of a 20-facility group in California. It's a "boutique" funeral home—just 6,000 square feet—created to serve the Danville community, which is an affluent group of Boomers. The nearest funeral homes are about 15 miles away on either side because Wilson & Kratzer is in the middle of what used to be farmland. They're in an exclusive, newly developed area with home values averaging about $500,000 and household income averaging about $125,000 a year.

When they came to town, Wilson & Kratzer purchased the former library of the town of Danville and did a complete renovation. The facility is open and bright with lots of windows—very unlike the old traditional funeral home. They have no pews. No organ. No piano. (CDs and satellite-fed music are played over an elaborate sound system or live musicians are brought in.)

"We're doing a lot of services that focus on personalization and memorialization," says Wilson & Kratzer's Dennis Steiner. "We find that many families here don't want to focus on the body. Often they have a private family viewing time followed by cremation or burial then a memorial or celebration service without the body present. The cremation rate here is about 65%."

Steiner reports that in lieu of the focus on the body, families want to celebrate the unique lifestyle of the person who died. During the arrangement conference they spend a lot of time gathering information about the person who died. Time is not a constraint. If they need to spend four or five hours with the family up-front, they do that. Then they use all that information to help the family create a very personalized funeral experience.

Wilson & Kratzer's funeral directors also facilitate the services for non-religious families. "I sense that more and more funeral directors may have to step into that role in the future," says Steiner. (See Ritual Specialist.)

At Wilson & Kratzer, "personalized funeral experiences" can mean almost anything. They deliver blank memory boards to the family's home so the family can assemble them and bring them back to the chapel for display. (Staff shows families sample memory boards to help them get ideas.) They do lots of dove and balloon releases.

They also "set the scene" for the service by creating a personalized visual environment. For example, they've done services for horse lovers where they've set the casket atop hay bales and placed a saddle on top of the casket instead of flowers. The rider's cowboy hat and boots were displayed nearby. They've also done fishing themes.

"A neighbor of mine collected hats," says Steiner. "When she died we displayed many of them around the gathering room, and in the obituary we invited all ladies attending the funeral to wear a hat or bonnet. It was quite moving to stand at the back of the room and see all those hats."

For a quilter's funeral, Wilson & Kratzer draped a quilt over the casket and hung others around the gathering room. After a young man's death they displayed his skis, his surfboard, his boat, his car and other items. They also blew up photos of him to lifesize and placed them around the gathering room. When a 45-year-old UPS driver died, they displayed his collection of UPS paraphernalia. They also scattered some of his ashes over his bocce ball court in his backyard and released 100 balloons for him at sunset. For an individual who loved redwood trees, they brought in 15-gallon potted trees and displayed them along with his personal belongings. Wilson & Kratzer's staff later planted the trees at the wife's property.

"We invite families to open up their thought processes and really personalize the service and honor the lifestyle of the person who died," explains Steiner.

Wilson & Kratzer also has a graphic artist on staff. They have set up a room for her with computers and other graphics equipment so she can create quite elaborate programs. She can scan photos, crop them, create collages, overlay text—whatever a family wants. They're able to receive photos e-mailed by family or our other branches to create programs. Families can choose the paper and the fonts and assist in the text if they wish.

For a NASCAR driver's funeral, for example, their graphics person used many photos of him with his cars and trophies. At the memorial service for a father who died suddenly of a heart attack, his 7-year-old daughter drew pictures which were incorporated in the memorial program.

These full-color programs give people something personal and special to walk away from the service with and contribute greatly to the Experience.

In designing their facility, Wilson & Kratzer created flexible spaces to meet a variety of needs. Their funeral home is rather small, with a main gathering room and two visitation rooms that can be opened up to create a larger reception room with adjoining kitchen facilities.

As you know, in the old days people had the gatherings at their homes and friends brought food over. But now, because of the inconvenience of preparing food at home, cleaning the house, etc., families often really like the idea of having the reception in their facility. Wilson & Kratzer often arranges for the catering, which can be simple or very elaborate.

"We had one that was a full-blown catered event for 100 people with gourmet hors d'oeuvres and a full kitchen and wait staff—$75 dollars a head," says Steiner. "And because we are near the wine country, we sometimes have requests for wine service at the reception in addition to the standard coffee, iced tea and soda."

"We find that it's very refreshing for families to come into our facility, where we're open and progressive, and invite them to be the same," Steiner emphasizes. "They may have encountered funeral homes that weren't receptive to new ideas and to personalizing the service. They may have been told, 'No, we don't do that.' We do everything we possibly can to make the funeral or memorial service a memorable experience for everyone."

Dennis Steiner can be reached at (925) 820-2999 or dsteiner@carriageservices.com.

Leadership

Funeral service needs leaders right now. The leader, or visionary, is an excellent listener. Committees of employees are fine to a point, but vision is really a function of leadership style and activity. Funeral service has too many people who take claim to leading their funeral home without following through. If you truly want to be a leader, be present, practice what you preach, and inspire the people around you to create meaningful funeral Experiences for each and every family you service. Leadership doesn't occur when you are out on the golf course; leadership occurs when you are in the arrangement conference room helping each and every family create a meaningful, personalized funeral Experience.

Your employees will look to you for direction without even knowing they are doing so. Your success or failure come from both what you have learned in your years in funeral service and what type of person you have become since early childhood. Stand up and be proud of your capacity to lead! Or, if you cannot or do not want to lead, put someone in management who can and will.

Listening

How can you provide excellent customer service without ever saying a word? By listening, really listening, to what your customers are saying.

Your job is to listen to those you are honored to serve. You must demonstrate a desire to understand and be responsive to their unique needs. You must be aware of both verbal and non-verbal signals they give you. You must find out not only what the family wants and needs to make for a meaningful funeral Experience, but what they don't want. One great way to determine what families may want and don't want is to ask them, "Have you ever seen something done at a funeral that you really liked? Disliked?"

Like the most sensitive receptors, you must be on what some people call "high receive." Even the quiet remark made by someone in the arrangement conference may offer clues to a way you can bring meaning to the funeral Experience.

Ask questions that assist you in your efforts to understand. Listen carefully and with attention to detail. Don't mentally wander even when someone is talking about something you may already know (e.g. the cause of the death, which clergy person will facilitate the ceremony, or what cemetery will be used.) Don't interrupt when others are talking. Allow, even encourage, times of silence for people to gather their thoughts. Give your undivided attention.

Personal Qualities of An Effective Listener

Desire. Perhaps the single most important characteristic of the good listener is desire. While this sounds simplistic, you need to want to listen. Remember—people can quickly detect a superficial desire to listen.

Commitment. An effective listener not only needs to have a general desire to listen, but also needs to be committed to the task of listening. To be committed means to be responsible. If you are unable to talk at a particular time, be honest. Share your desire to talk and arrange for another time.

Patience. In addition to desire and commitment, the listening funeral director needs to have patience. If you are in a hurry and are anxious to get the situation "taken care of," chances are that you will do a poor job of listening. Be patient and available to provide the understanding bereaved families seek from you.

Another facet of listening patience is learning that you do not need to fill every silence. There is a time for speaking and a time for silence. Sometimes in your effort to help, you may feel the need to keep the conversation going. Discipline yourself and remember: Listening also involves listening to the silent moments as the other person struggles to express a feeling or pauses to consider a thought.

Attending—Listening's Cohort

Listening with your ears is just one part of truly listening. Listening with your body, or what I call attending, further communicates your desire to help bereaved families. Body language such as eye contact, posture, physical distance, facial expression, gesture, tone of voice, rate of speech, and energy level all communicate something about your ability to listen. Even seemingly superficial characteristics such as physical appearance and setting make a difference.

When you learn that more than two-thirds of all communication takes place through non-verbal means, you can understand the importance of developing attending skills.

Eye contact. Perhaps the most effective way of making contact with people, especially shortly after a death, is to look them in the eye as you talk with them. While you certainly do not have to maintain a fixed stare, the appropriate procedure is to look at the people you are helping both while they are talking with you and during times of silence. Also, don't ignore people who by their nature or current emotional state are very quiet. You still want to make eye contact with them to help them feel included and supported. Of course, eye contact means different things to people of different cultures. Keep this important caveat in mind as you as you work with customers of various cultural backgrounds.

Posture. A second component of attending is posture. Each moment of every day, we communicate a great deal by how we stand, sit and walk. Take a moment right now to become aware of your posture and what it might communicate to someone entering the room. Interested listeners lean into a conversation and are relaxed in posture; disinterested or unfriendly listeners lean away from the speaker and fold their arms across their chests. Can you picture the difference?

Physical distance. In general, physical closeness demonstrates a desire to help. Use the other bereaved person's reaction as a guide. If he or she draws back, take that as an indication that you are too close. We have found that most people are comfortable talking at a distance of about three feet. Try to arrange seating to take advantage of this.

Facial expression. The expression on your face should match, as closely as possible, the emotional tone of what is occurring around you. Few people are more aware of the importance of this than those involved in funeral service. Your facial expressions can easily communicate a sense of warmth, as well as the message, "I am with you, I understand, and I want to help you." You may find that you communicate something differently with your facial expression than you are aware. After all, to see your facial expression is difficult unless you look in a mirror. You might want to ask your family, friends, and co-workers how they perceive your different expressions.

Gesture. You communicate much not only through your posture, but through your body movements. Your gestures should be natural and not interfere with your intended communication. If you move quickly or have mannerisms that are distracting, you will take a great deal away from your ability to help. Ask yourself if your gestures communicate what you are trying to communicate.

Poor attending behaviors tend to stop conversation or prohibit a helping relationship from being established. If you find yourself unable to pay attention effectively over a period of time, you will most likely notice some changes in the family's behavior. They may become passive and have difficulty in sharing their hurt in a mutual relationship. The result is that you'll probably move into a question/answer pattern difficult to get out of. On the other hand, they may become upset, impatient, and angry because you do not appear interested and concerned. These are signs that your attending skills are lacking and indicate that the person is not satisfied with the level of attention you are offering.

Location

As you may know, one trend we are seeing in funeral service today is more families requesting to hold services in locations other than the funeral home or place of worship (church, synagogue, temple, etc.). If you are listening to and responding to this need for creative personalization and memorialization, this trend suggests you will be holding more services in a variety of settings.

Obviously, there are a myriad of ways to personalize funerals, but one excellent way is to hold the funeral in a meaningful location other than places of worship or the funeral home. This is often particularly appropriate for non-religious families, but even deeply religious services can be held in atypical locations if the family and the funeral officiant are so inclined. If you open your heart and mind to this concept, you'll see that funerals and memorial services can be held almost anywhere—parks, football fields, homes, riverbanks, horse barns. Almost any place that holds special meaning for the family and friends of the person who died is appropriate. As you'll learn from the stories of three funerals that follow, for some families the location of the funeral can make all the difference in the world.

Jack Bauer of Bauer Funeral Home, Incorporated was good enough to share these stories with me. Bauer Funeral Home is located in Kittanning, Pennsylvania, a small community north of Pittsburgh. The business was started in 1947 by Jack's father and now his daughter, Jennifer, who's 25, works there as a licensed funeral director, too. They serve about 140 families a year in a draw area of about 16,000 people. Mostly their families still request old-fashioned, traditional funerals. Last year just 8% chose cremation.

A few years ago, Bauer Funeral Home orchestrated three particularly interesting funerals in three unique locations. In the first, Jennifer, a champion figure skater who was a senior in high school, died in a car crash.

"When I went to the house to talk with the family, the aunt answered the door and said, 'Now I want you to understand—they don't want a funeral and they don't want to talk to you.'," explains Jack. "Understandably, this family was very upset. With the aunt's help, I was finally able to begin talking with the parents. They said they didn't want a funeral because they didn't want to hurt the kids at Jennifer's school. They wanted direct cremation, even though in our community we traditionally have two evenings' visitation."

After Jack talked with them for a while, they agreed to have one evening's visitation, which turned out to be a very healing experience for all. For the funeral service itself, Jack had been thinking about the fact that this family wasn't attached to a church. What location did hold meaning for them? Since Jennifer was a competitive figure skater, they spent hours and hours every week at the local ice arena. Jack suggested to them that they could hold a service at the ice rink. Within minutes the parents had not only embraced the idea but were coming up with many other ideas of their own.

During the ceremony, 30 skaters from the skating team were seated on the ice. Jennifer's coaches displayed her trophies. Jennifer's mom and dad sat in the bleachers where they always sat to watch Jennifer skate. The arena holds about 700 people and it was filled to capacity.

"We gave every kid in attendance a red rose to place on the ice at the end of the ceremony," says Jack. "Then Jennifer's mom and dad walked onto the ice. Jennifer's mom placed her white rose on top of the mound of red roses then knelt down, kissed her hand and stroked the ice with her hand, mouthing the words 'Goodbye.' This was a very touching, emotional service and it had a tremendous impact on the entire community."

Jack also held a funeral on a tennis court in 1999 for an older tennis buff who lived in his community. She played tennis all the time—well into her 80s—and the town named the court on which she played Maude Maize Tennis Court. When she died last winter, Jack called her relatives, who lived out of state. She had no children, just nieces and nephews, and they requested direct cremation. But Jack and the family agreed that in the spring, they would hold a memorial service for Maude. So when the weather started getting nicer, he called them back and suggested they hold her service on her tennis court. The family loved the idea. They created a simple ceremony in memory of Maude.

"With about 40 of us seated on the tennis court," Jack explains, "they read scripture and shared stories for an hour and a half. They also released helium balloons. Then we served punch and cookies right there. It was so fitting."

The third unique service location Jack hit upon was the country club. A local doctor's wife had died. He said he was an atheist and that he wanted direct cremation. Jack persuaded him that since he and his wife, Brownie, had so many friends in this community and had lived there for so long, he should have some sort of gathering in her honor. Finally they decided on a reception to be held two days later at the country club. Jack also asked the doctor to bring him 25-30 photos of Brownie from throughout her life for a video memorial tribute.

"My daugther and I put together an order of service for the reception," says Jack. "We told some stories about her and invited others to do the same. Then we showed the video and darned if the doctor didn't stand up and start narrating Brownie's life story. He talked about each photo of her as it appeared on the screen. And then he proceeded to lead the rest of the service himself. At the end of the service, we all toasted Brownie while singing Auld Lang Syne."

Congratulations, Jack, on having helped create three meaningful Experiences where there might have been none at all. If you hadn't taken the lead in suggesting a different venue for each of these services, these families and this community would not have been helped to heal through the power of personalized ceremony. Jack found that the different funeral locations move the funeral away from the so-called "establishment" funeral homes, which are places many of today's families don't want to be. In each of these three cases, suggesting a different locale opened the door to a whole new world of ideas for these families.

"A child in my community once said to one of my children, 'Your daddy gives parties for dead people.',," Jack concludes. "That's so true. Bauer Funeral Home does give parties—complete with all the personalized touches. Parties are all about the Experience. And we're open to having these parties anywhere the family would like to. Funerals always require organization and dignity, but beyond that, the sky's the limit."

Jack Bauer can be reached at bauerfh@alltel.net.

Manners

If your staff has poor manners, all you do to create exceptional funeral Experiences for today's families will be in vain. Good basic manners sometimes seem old-fashioned, but they do make a huge difference to contemporary customers.

Do you open doors for customers? Take and hang up their coats? Make eye contact? Shake hands when you first meet? Offer beverages? Walk customers to the right room (including restrooms) instead of pointing when they don't know the way? Say please and thank you and excuse me?

Another facet of good manners involves respect—speaking to and acting respectfully in front of families. Treat all family members—young and old—as you would your boss or your grandmother: with respect. I've noticed that some funeral directors aren't very good at ascertaining the family's emotional tone. They're glib or overly casual when the family is clearly distraught. Or, conversely, they're overly somber or lackluster when the family is clearly enthusiastic about planning a personalized funeral Experience.

Spend a few minutes observing the manners of your staff today. You might be surprised that even long-term employees don't always have the best manners; not everyone was raised with them. Follow up by having a staff meeting and role playing your expectations for good manners.

Media

Being an available, articulate spokesperson for funeral service with the local media will enhance your standing in the community, educate area citizenry and ultimately make for better funeral Experiences for everyone involved.

To help you understand the fundamentals of dealing with the media, I asked Joe Weigel, Director of Marketing and Corporate Communications for Batesville Casket Company, to provide us with some tips. He says that the best way to generate positive media coverage is to work WITH local television, radio and newspaper reporters and editors. "It's one of the best ways of reaching families outside your normal means," he says.

Media relations is the rapport you establish with journalists and how those relationships affect the news coverage your firm receives. It's ultra-critical because the media filters and then delivers your message to the public. And, your goal is to make that message as positive as possible.

Building a relationship with the media

You can achieve good, positive media attention, according to Weigel, but only if you're willing to invest in building relationships with reporters and editors. You may wish to select one person at your firm to handle all media relations. When the media calls, politely refer their calls to this person without sounding defensive. The media will come to trust this person and, eventually, his story suggestions. The best route to possible coverage is to prove you're a worthy subject and a reliable source.

The easiest way to start is by becoming acquainted with editors and reporters. That doesn't mean pestering them when they're on deadline or parking yourself outside their offices. If it's convenient, stop by and introduce yourself, your firm and drop off a press kit. Be sure to note deadlines and don't visit then. You may wish to phone or e-mail in advance and schedule a brief meeting. Or, send a warm cover note with your press kit then follow-up with a phone call or e-mail.

"The key is to be accessible," says Weigel. "After the first visit or communication, periodically call or submit legitimate story or column ideas. Don't neglect to briefly follow-up after each submission to make sure the journalist received the idea or release and gauge their interest. Guise your request by asking if they'd like more information."

Once an editor or reporter has used an idea or news release in a story, continue to pass along others. This establishes you as a credible source, one whom the journalist can trust. Make it easy for the reporter or editor by supplying interesting stories with all of the pertinent information and your chances of coverage improve significantly.

If a reporter calls you

If a reporter calls to interview you on a funeral service-related topic, be professional, positive, concise and genuine. Always tell the truth. If you don't know the answer, offer to research it and call back. If you're uncomfortable with a question, say so, but try to direct your answer positively. Avoid the "no comment" response if at all possible. When you don't respond, it appears you have something to hide. Respect and answer simple questions. Remember, the point is to educate the public—via this reporter—about funeral service.

For more tips on writing news releases, submitting article and column ideas, preparing a press kit and more, call Joe Weigel at (812) 934-1610.

Memories

This is what it's all about, folks. Remembering the person who died. Eliciting and embracing memories. Reminiscing. Honoring a unique person's life. If the funerals you help create don't do these things, you're not creating Experiences for families and you're not getting the point.

The good news is that there are a myriad of opportunities for families to integrate memories into the funeral Experience beyond the eulogy. Some creative alternatives include:

Memory baskets: Provide a place where people can write down memories on paper and place them in a "memory basket." Some of these memories can be incorporated into the eulogy.

Memory books: Convert your registration book into a registration/memory book. Leave a column on the right-hand side of the registration book and encourage people to not only sign their names, but to write out a memory or two of the person who has died. Families often want multiple copies so that they can each have a copy of this memory book. You have just added value to the service you provide.

Memory tables or memory boards: Many funeral homes make available tables or boards for families to place memorabilia and pictures. These "linking objects" often give people a safe place to gather and share memories of the person who died. Please note that memory tables and memory boards are the BARE MINIMUM effort to help families remember the person who died. They're wonderful tools but don't think they're adequate to create an exceptional Experience.

Memory videos: Some funeral homes offer memory videos that incorporate visual images with music. There are a growing number of companies that can provide you with this service.

Personalized programs: Wilson & Kratzer Funeral Home (see Innovation) creates personalized programs full of photos for every family it serves. In fact, think of programs as mini-biographies in addition to explanations of the order of service and you're getting the picture. All it takes is a scanner, a computer, a printer, software and a little practice and you, too, can be publishing amazing programs destined to become family heirlooms.

Holiday memory services: Many funeral homes offer ways to give testimony to memories during the holiday season. (See Holidays.)

Memorial Day programs: Some funeral homes sponsor services around the Memorial Day holiday, giving families served an opportunity to do memory work.

Memorial candle-lighting ceremonies: A wonderful way to reach out to your community is to hold an annual candle-lighting ceremony in memory of those who have died.

Get creative as you brainstorm ways to help families remember the person who died. After all, this is the stuff that Experiences are made of.

Micro-managing

Let me share with you John's story. John, 42, had been managing his second generation, midwestern funeral home for eight years when he purchased two additional funeral homes. With the new purchases, his business went from serving approximately 350 families a year to 525 families a year.

While this growth sounds great, John has a problem: He's a micro-manager. He has his hands in all aspects of the operation of all three funeral homes. "I've always had a tendency to do the things I've hired other people to do," says John. "I got this management characteristic honestly. My father modeled it for me for 30 years. He did removals, made arrangements with almost every family we served, was present at all visitations, paid all the bills, and even cut the grass."

Like his father before him, John now finds himself too involved in every aspect of the funeral homes he is trying to grow. The paradox is, the more he micro-manages, the more he inhibits the ultimate growth of his business.

John is not alone. There appears to be a multitude of micro-managers in funeral service today. After all, that's how many funeral homes got their start. New owners got involved in every part of the daily goings-on at the funeral home. While learning all the small details of the funeral home's operations is helpful during the first part of the learning curve, it can be very detrimental as a long-term management style.

For some owner/managers of funeral homes, this style of management could almost be termed a genetic disorder. In other words, it gets passed down generationally from parent to child, primarily through modeling of what I call "Funeral Service Worktapes" (see W for Worktapes).

These worktapes are mostly subconscious messages about work that are stored away in the recesses of the brain. The problem is that worktapes often put you at risk for being a micro-manager. Examples include:

- "If you want something done right, do it yourself."
- "If you are resting, you are lazy."
- "Be available at all times."

The problem is that these worktapes take over to the point that they control your entire work style and personal life. It's as if the mind plays them over and over again, but at a level so deep that the conscious mind cannot easily articulate them.

Many funeral homes are breeding grounds for micro-management. The personality, style, and work ethic of the founding owner/operator often created the very success the funeral home is now enjoying. Yet, as a funeral home grows, micro-management can send the wrong message to both families served and employees.

Communicating the Wrong Message To Families Served and Employees

Too much attention to detail can send the wrong message to both families and employees. Families may sense that the owner/manager doesn't trust employees to do a good job of serving them. Moreover, the fear that the micro-manager has of delegating important responsibilities sometimes results in staff not having the information or skills they need to effectively serve families.

Micro-managers also stunt the growth of individual employees. The classic example is the employee who wants to be able to make funeral arrangements with families, but is never, or infrequently, allowed to. Unable to grow in their work role, they eventually look for other job opportunities.

The resentment that employees experience when they are not trusted to do their jobs puts the funeral home at risk for high turnover. A business is very much like a garden. The individual plants will find it impossible to grow if they are shaded from the sun by the always-present shadow of the gardener.

High Risk For Burn-Out

Micro-managers often claim to enjoy and even "feed on" the stress that results from their attention to detail. However, the long-term consequence threatens their well-being, leading to:

- exhaustion and loss of energy.
- irritability and impatience.
- cynicism and detachment.
- physical complaints and depression.
- disorientation and confusion.

- feelings of omnipotence and indispensibility.
- minimization and denial of feelings.

It may take a while for Type A micro-managers to really burn out, but burn out they will. And in the meantime they will have compromised their personal lives, their family's lives and even the long-term well-being of their own company.

Missing the Big Picture

An additional consequence is the lack of time for more visionary leadership tasks, such as long-term planning. Micro-managers often miss the big picture. They are so busy with all of the details that they don't have time to slow down and actively do strategic planning. The irony is that they frequently talk about the need to reorganize and do better planning for the future.

Ten Symptoms of Micro-Management

Take inventory of your tendency to micro-manage. Do you:

1. Believe your employees can never live up to your standards.

2. Fear the delegation of important responsibilities.

3. Find yourself frequently reviewing employees' work.

4. Make the arrangements with the majority of families you serve (of course, this depends on the number of families you serve).

5. Feel the need to be seen at every visitation or service.

6. Feel guilty when you take a vacation, or take no vacation at all. (After all, who could you leave in charge to manage all the details?)

7. Find yourself unable to find time to write out your funeral home's long-term business plan.

8. Tend to worry a lot about the funeral home even when things are going well.

9. Notice that your family and friends complain that you spend so much more time with the funeral home than with them.

10. Rationalize that your "business" just comes with the job of funeral service.

Overcoming Micro-Management

All change begins with insight. An important step toward more balanced management is to understand what underlies the behavior. Ask yourself: "Do I have some 'funeral service worktapes' that are driving me to micro-manage?" Slow down and consciously listen to your worktapes.

The true test of a funeral home owner/manager is not what he or she can do, rather it is what his or her people can do without him or her. Can they plan and carry out meaningful funerals for families served? Can they respond to unusual requests? Can they solve problems? A well-managed funeral home can operate successfully in the temporary or permanent absence of any given manager. Determine which tasks only you can do (and be brutally honest with yourself here!), then distribute the rest of the work to others with specific direction and expectations, and then **let them do it.**

Resist the temptation to get absorbed in all the detailed workings of the funeral home. Stop thinking you must give your attention to every detail. While delegating will be difficult at first, it's a time-wise decision for achieving time-management and long-term planning goals.

As you work to change your micro-management workstyle, ask yourself, "What is the best use of my time right now?" Remember, it's easy to look and feel busy without being effective. What's important is to retrain yourself to do what matters most in terms of effective use of your time.

If you are a longtime micro-manager, realize there is no quick fix! It took John, our micro-manager from the beginning of the piece, a bout with health problems and a near-trip to divorce court to realize the error of his ways. But he has, over the course of a year and after much introspection, learned to delegate effectively and is today managing a much healthier, happier business.

Misconceptions

As I travel across North America each year, I encounter many misconceptions about funerals. Here are a few of them. I hope you'll join me in refuting them whenever you have the chance.

- **Funerals are too expensive.**
  The social, psychological and emotional benefits of authentic funerals far outweigh their financial costs. Besides, a funeral needn't be lavishly expensive to be meaningful.

- **Funerals make us too sad.**
  When someone loved dies, we need to be sad. Funerals provide us with a safe place in which to embrace our pain.

- **Funerals are barbaric.**
  On the contrary, meaningful funeral ceremonies are civilized, socially binding rituals. Some people think that viewing the body is barbaric. Cultural differences aside, viewing has many benefits for survivors.

- **Funerals are inconvenient.**
  Taking a few hours out of your week to demonstrate your love for the person who died and your support for survivors is not an inconvenience but a privilege.

- **Funerals and cremation are mutually exclusive.**
  A funeral (with or without the body present) may be held prior to cremation. Embalmed bodies are often cremated.

- **Funerals require the body to be embalmed.**
  Not necessarily. Depending on local regulations, funerals held shortly after the death may require no special means of preservation.

- **Funerals are only for religious people.**
  Not true. Non-religious ceremonies (which, by the way, need not be held in a church or officiated by a clergy person) can still meet the survivors' mourning needs.

- **Funerals are rote and meaningless.**
  They needn't be. With forethought and planning, funerals can and should be personalized rituals reflecting the uniqueness of the bereaved family.

- **Funerals should reflect what the dead person wanted.**
  Not really . . . While pre-planning your funeral may help you reconcile yourself to your own mortality, funerals are primarily for the benefit of the living.

- **Funerals are only for grown-ups.**
  Anyone old enough to love is old enough to mourn. Children, too, have the right and the privilege to attend funerals.

Motivation

People in ownership or management have the opportunity to help influence outstanding performance that benefits not only those you serve, but also the individual employee and everyone who hopes to have a future in funeral service. Let's explore the three keys to motivation.

Recognition

Recognition means acknowledging excellent work when you observe it. Regardless of how self-motivated a funeral director is, it is usually appreciated when others take notice. If you have ever worked in an environment where there is never any positive recognition from ownership or management, you know that employee morale can suffer.

Ideas for Recognizing Excellent Work for Funeral Directors:

• Ask a funeral director who has strengths in a certain area (arranging conference skills, embalming) to present an inservice to other employees.

• Post thank-you letters from families who have been well-served.

• Give hand-written notes to recognize outstanding work.

• Right after observing exceptional service, let the funeral director know you noticed and valued his efforts.

• Provide continuing education opportunities to good performers. Enhanced knowledge and skill can be very rewarding.

These are but a few ideas for recognizing employee performance. Do keep in mind, however, that what is motivating for one person may not be motivating for another. Vary your means of recognition depending on the individual.

Responsibility

To inspire excellent work performance, funeral directors must be given responsibility, for it is responsibility that creates involvement and investment in one's work. Responsibility encourages employees to make their work the best that it can be—to strive for excellence.

Ideas for Giving Responsibility to Funeral Directors:

- *Build their skills and abilities to take an increasing share of responsibility for work.* For example, have you ever witnessed a funeral director who wants to make arrangements with families but is never given the training or opportunity to do so? You will never get exceptional work from funeral directors if you don't provide them increased responsibilities and encourage their personal and professional growth.

- *After you observe skills in certain areas of work performance, increase responsibilities within that area.* For example, you may have a staff member who is skilled with computers. Delegate responsibility to establish and oversee the computer systems operations of the funeral home. Or you discover a gifted speaker on your staff. Encourage this employee to represent the funeral home at speaking engagements in your service area.

- *Create boundaries for ownership of work.* How much latitude can an employee have without seeking additional management approval? For example, a family makes an unusual service request (e.g., "We would like to bring his (the deceased's) dog into the funeral home to say good-bye to him"). Can the funeral director respond to this request on his own, or must he seek management approval? As competence increases, expand the boundaries of decision-making that the employee can be responsible for.

- *Trust the funeral director to do excellent work.* Trust is an excellent motivator. Trust that you don't have to look over his shoulder constantly or always double-check his work performance. If the funeral director doesn't feel you trust him, you will not get inspired work.

Again, these are but a few ideas for giving responsibility to employees in the funeral home. What additional examples can you think of?

Reward

Reward goes beyond financial compensation. The funeral home has a right to expect good work from employees who are paid to provide services. However, excellent work can also be rewarded in other ways.

Ideas for Rewarding Funeral Directors for Exceptional Work Performance:

- Modest rewards, such as a gift certificate for dinner out or concert or ball game tickets, are often very appreciated.

- Providing additional time-off as scheduling allows, such as a weekend off.

- Sending an employee to attend your state Funeral Directors' Association conference or the annual NFDA convention.

- Taking an employee to lunch occasionally is a simple, yet appropriate way to let hem know he is appreciated.

- Gatherings during holidays or birthday parties are a nice way to say thank you.

- Rewarding an employee with a trip away after so many years of service and excellent work performance can be an excellent motivator.

WARNING—Be careful not to reward the wrong things. I recently learned of a misguided funeral home that rewarded funeral directors for how quickly and how many families they could make arrangements with. Never make the mistake of confusing efficiency with effectiveness.

Niche

One of the must important aspects of differentiating your funeral home from other funeral homes (and third party providers) is to find and project a particular image for your business—an image different enough to be unique yet still credible. To achieve this goal, you must find your niche, the way in which families served see your funeral home as being special.

With today's new customer, your niche may just as well be defined by the meaningful funeral Experiences you help families create as by the uniqueness and quality of your products.

Better yet, how about combining the two? Unique, personalized funeral Experiences with unique personalized products.

Obstacles

I often do inservice trainings for funeral home staffs on a variety of topics. During a recent training, one funeral director was determined to project his uncomfortableness with the need for the very changes I was exploring with the staff.

As I described the "new customer" as outlined in Chapter 2 of this book, he kept interrupting and talking about all the obstacles to serving these people. He ranted and raved, "It will take too long to make arrangements to create these personalized funerals you are talking about."

Obviously, this funeral director has no real desire to adapt and change with the new customer. He has no desire to create meaningful funeral Experiences. He is what I would call a functionary, not a facilitator.

Invariably, when you try to implement change in the funeral home, obstacles will arise. Among them are staffers like:

1. The skeptic who tries to distract you from making changes.

2. The complainer who whines, "But it will take longer." (They confuse the good E's with the bad E's.)

3. The passive-aggresive who tries to procrastinate or show you down or outright sabotage changes you are trying to make.

Count on some human obstacles; just don't let them keep you from making necessary changes.

People

At a recent workshop I taught on self-care in funeral service, a funeral director friend said to me, "Funeral service would be great if it weren't for the people."

Yes, my friend is burned-out and questioning his future in funeral service. He has been seeing too many bereaved families and working too many hours. He has been neglecting his own family relationships and feels disconnected from both friends and family.

Supportive relationships are necessary for everyone, funeral directors included. The capacity to have meaningful friendships and intimate family relationships is vital to your well-being. Many funeral directors are better at giving than receiving. Yet, if you neglect your personal relationships as you commit yourself to your chosen vocation, you may end up lonely, depressed, and frustrated.

Focusing on the needs of families you serve is important; however, you may be at risk for losing touch with yourself. Or, as my friend went on to say, "I feel like a stranger to myself. I'm just going through the motions and I know the families I'm trying to help can tell my heart isn't in it. I don't have time for my friends, my family, or for me."

Now, usually this funeral director is excellent at supporting and even nurturing families he serves. Actually, he is what I call a "natural nurturer." Interestingly enough, we know that nurturers are often in need of intimacy, nurturance and support themselves. It appears that natural nurturers often give other people what they unconsciously know they need themselves.

Too much giving and caring for others without good self-care-breaks can and often does result in burnout for very good funeral directors. Discovering the balance between giving and receiving can be a fragile see-saw. Sometimes it is learned through mistakes of over-giving and over-working.

Funeral Directors Need Intimate, Supportive Relationships

The demands of funeral service leave some funeral directors feeling as if they already spend enough time with people. Sometime, you may feel like you don't have any energy left for socializing with friends and family. Yet, staying balanced and having joy in your life requires meaningful relationships. There is a lot of truth in the old maxim "No man is an island unto himself."

Family and friend relationships are where most people look for fulfillment of their needs for support and intimacy. Yet, many funeral directors report to me that they feel lonely and isolated from family and friends. This is a "red flag" symptom that the funeral director is spending too much time at work and not enough time at home. If this sounds familiar to you, read on.

This may be a time when you need to open yourself up to personal relationships in new ways by enhancing your relationships of giving and receiving or deepening the existing relationships in your life.

Many funeral directors who suffer from loneliness and isolation are over-committed and struggle with cutting back and learning to say no. The paradox is that the more you over-give to work, the more distant you will feel from family and friends. You deserve the time and energy it requires to listen to and attend to yourself and those you love deeply. You need to let go of the pretense that you are a limitless source of nurturance to others.

Caring for yourself, your family and friends is an integral part of self-love. It may be time for you to break free from an overly serious approach to life, and laugh, have fun, play more, and make a conscious choice to cultivate joy in your life.

Many funeral directors have internalized the funeral service worktape that drones, "Work always comes first. Take care of others, not yourself." If you live this out, you will be at risk for becoming outwardly directed and lose connection with your inner world.

If the thoughts in this section are ringing a bell for you, take action now. Right now you can decide to work on being more connected to your family and friends. If you feel you are in a cycle you cannot get out of (working too much, no time for family, can't say no, etc.), care enough about yourself to seek professional counsel. Seeking help doesn't mean you are weak. Actually, it means you want to rediscover joy for life and value yourself, your family, and your friends. Again, remember, you are not an island!

Personalizing

Funerals should be personalized tributes to the person who died.

That bears repeating.

Funerals should be personalized tributes to the person who died.

It is your job to help families think about the qualities of the person who died and what this person meant to others and then USE this information to create a personalized ceremony. Consider his or her passions, hobbies, pasttimes, likes, dislikes. How can you help this family capture this unique life?

Be creative as you, together with the family and the person who will lead the service, brainstorm how to remember and honor the person who died.

Don't forget to discuss:

- Attributes or passions of the person who died that the family wants to be sure to honor.
- Special memories to share.
- Important people to include somehow.
- Person to lead the ceremony.
- Others who might want to speak or share memories.
- Honorary roles at the funeral:
  - *Pallbearears*
  - *Readers*
  - *Honorary pallbearers*
  - *Singer/musicians*
  - *Ushers*
- Music ideas for the visitation.
- Music ideas for the ceremony.
- Readings ideas for the ceremony.
- Personal items that could be displayed (at the visitation, the service and/or the gathering afterwards): Photos, collections, hobby paraphernalia, artwork and many other objects that tangibly depict the life of the person who died are meaningful and appropriate to display.

John Kane of R.S. Kane Funeral Home in Ontario related several ideas he has used for peronalizing the service. For one funeral, the son mentioned that his father had been in the 48th Highlanders Regiment. Together they decided that a bagpiper would be appropriate and that the father's jacket, which had very special buttons, should be on display in the visitation room rather than the casket as first planned. For an ardent golfer, the funeral home's floral designer was given the golf bag to use as a "vase." This arrangement was placed at the head of the casket. For a young man who loved his red, custom-built car, the funeral director suggested parking the car near the funeral home's front door on the day of the service. The engine was revved as people left. John himself led the funeral procession on his Harley for a friend's funeral.

If you truly listen to families and are genuinely interested in learning about the person who died, they will tell you what you need to know to help them personalize the service. Pick up on their cues and make creative suggestions.

Some Ideas to Offer to Families in Helping Them Personalize a Funeral Service

As you are meeting with the family, emphasize that the funeral service they have should be as special as the life they will be remembering. Here are a few ideas:

• Write a personalized obituary. Some newspapers allow you to express a little more than the usual who/what/why/where/when. Appoint a creative "word" person in the family to handle this task.

• Create a column in the guest book for people to jot down a memory after they sign their name.

• Display personal items or hobby paraphernalia on a table at the visitation, the ceremony and/or the gathering afterwards.

• Have more than one person deliver the eulogy. Ask several people to share memories and talk about different aspects of the person who died.

• Choose clothing for the person who died that reflects his or her life, interests, passions, etc. The clothing needn't be formal or somber!

• Create a personalized program for the ceremony. You can include photos, poems, anecdotes—whatever you'd like! Your funeral director can help you with this.

• Show a videotape or slide show of the person's life during the funeral. Pictures tell a thousand words!

- Ask children if they would like to write a letter or draw a picture for the person who died. Their "goodbyes" can then be placed in the casket alongside the body.

- Select flowers that were meaningful to the person who died. A simple arrangement of freshly-cut lilacs, for example, might be perfect.

- At the funeral, invite people to write down a memory of the person who died. Appoint someone to gather and read the memories aloud.

- Create a funeral that captures the personality of the person who died. If he was zany, don't be afraid to use humor. If she was affectionate, have everyone stand up and hug the person next to them during the ceremony.

- Display photos of the person who died at the visitation, the ceremony and/or the gathering. In fact, putting together a photo collage can be a very healing experience for the family in the days before the funeral.

- Use lots of music, especially if music was meaningful to the person who died or is to your family. Music can be played at the visitation, the committal service and the gathering as well as the funeral service itself!

- Create a personalized grave marker. Include a poem, a drawing or a short phrase that defines the person who died.

One more time:
Funerals should be personalized tributes to the person who died.

Planning

Have you ever noticed how customer service receives a great deal of lip-service in funeral service? Across the board, in both small and large funeral homes, family-owned and corporate, many people hold the timeless thought that the "customer is king." The majority of funeral directors—owners, manager, and front-line personnel alike—really do want to deliver excellent customer service. However, have you ever noticed that there is sometimes a gap between the desire to offer excellent service and the *performance* of that service?

So how does a well-intentioned funeral home move successfully from the desire to the performance? With a plan— an overall business plan and a service plan (what I'll call a service "strategy") to creating excellence in customer service.

The business plan ✓

It is vital to have an overall business plan for your funeral home, whether you serve 50 families a year or 500. In fact, with the current challenges facing funeral service it has probably never been more important to have a comprehensive business plan.

Which reminds me of a good story . . . A pilot announces to airline passengers, "I'm sorry to inform you that all our navigational instruments have ceased operation. We have no idea where we are headed. But we do seem to be making excellent time!"

If you don't know the route you're going, you may well get lost or spiral out of control.

Planning is the process that allows a funeral home to become what it wants to become. In part, the business plan is the identification of opportunities and the allocation of resources to make things happen in an orderly, progressive manner. It is about determining where you are now, where you want to be and how you plan to go about getting from here to there.

Here are just a few of the many benefits of creating an overall business plan for your funeral home:

- *Planning acknowledges the need to consider basic goals and policies of the funeral home.* Some funeral homes have not taken advantage of the opportunity to create a mission statement. Why was this funeral home established? What are the purposes and goals of this funeral home? What policies do we need to have in place to achieve these goals? Planning requires that you answer these questions and stay focused on why you are doing what you are doing. Perhaps you have observed that some funeral homes get in trouble because they move away from a customer-driven mission statement to a purely bottom-line, dollar-driven focus.

- *Planning creates the need for sound organizational structure.* As you plan the goals of your funeral home, you will clearly see the need to allocate staff to carry out each goal.

- *Planning mandates participation.* For the funeral home to achieve the established goals and objectives, all employees will have to cooperate. So wise planning helps create a teamwork environment. Everyone sees that they play an important role in the overall business plan. To focus on the importance of each member of the team is to focus on excellence in customer service.

- *Planning helps management strive for excellence.* Planning focuses attention on those things that influence the overall success of the funeral home. For example, if expected results are not achieved, the plan may need to be adjusted or changed. If outside variables such as trends toward increased numbers of dissatisfied customers affect the plan, management may need to consider personnel changes or increased staff training.

- *Planning mandates feedback and regularly scheduled reappraisal.* Planning helps the funeral home inventory progress toward achievement of goals and review potential problems that impede success. Feedback and reappraisal encourages constant fine-tuning to best meet the needs of the families you serve.

During this challenging time, "seat-of-the-pants" funeral home ownership and management will not suffice. To be successful into the next century, funeral homes must participate in a systematic planning process that includes regular update sessions. The funeral home must see to it that the business plan is kept current when conditions (such as increased direct cremation, new competition, death rate fluctuations, increased number of dissatisfied customers) change.

The funeral home that creates a well-considered business plan will provide itself with the direction necessary to be successful. In addition, the funeral home will be able to make necessary adjustments when conditions change and take advantage of new opportunities when they arise.

An inspiring slogan ✓

Bill McQueen of Anderson-McQueen Funeral Homes in St. Petersburg, Florida tells me that his staff provides excellent customer service by striving to make sure that everything they do is in alignment with their company's slogan: "Where compassionate professionals serve with integrity and distinction." His staff developed this theme and each word has a special meaning for them.

✓ *Compassionate* - Each staff member should feel the family's distress and work to alleviate it. We want to leave the family with an impression of us as caring, understanding, considerate and sympathetic.

✓ *Professional* - Each staff member should exhibit expert knowledge in his or her area of work, accuracy, efficient teamwork and consistent and persistent attention to detail.

✓ *Serve* - Basically, we are the family's "servant" during this time of need. No task is too small or too great for us to handle.

✓ *Integrity* - We strive to do what is right because it is right, even when it does not benefit us and even when the people we are serving are not even aware that we have done it.

• *Distinction* - We want to be clearly distinguishable from all the other funeral homes in the area so we try to do things with some flair. We have reviewed all areas of service and tried to find some acts of "customer surprise" that we can include in that function area that really pleases the customer (e.g. complimentary audiotape of every funeral service).

Anderson-McQueen has posted this slogan in all employee areas and asks every employee to memorize it. "We feel that if we only had one minute to train a new staff member, we would have him memorize the slogan," says Bill. "If he then dealt with any given set of circumstances based upon the parameters of the slogan, we know he would be giving great service!"

The service strategy

Developing a service strategy, which is a subset of the overall business plan, involves defining your potential customers, determining what their expectations are, and creating a match between your customers' expectations and your ability to deliver service. Operating a funeral home without a defined service strategy may have worked 25 years ago, but it won't work in today's changed environment and the evolution of the "never-satisfied customer." Without such a strategy, you don't know who your customers are and how much they value different aspects of the products and services you provide.

Still, when asked the question, "What is your service strategy?", many funeral directors say something like, "We don't really have one," "What do you mean—a service strategy?" or "We just know we provide great service."

Without a service strategy the funeral home is often not managed in a way to assure quality service, while a well-defined service strategy helps create high quality service standards. Funeral homes that have a clear, focused service strategy will be better prepared to be successful today, tomorrow, and well into the future.

While not all-inclusive, the questions that follow should help you develop a service strategy.

- Who are we currently serving?

- What types of services do these families want?

- Do we provide these services (and do them well)?

- Over the past decade, what customer trends can we identify?

- Who would we like to serve that we aren't right now?

- What needs does this group(s) have?

- How are we doing on five important service qualities—reliability, responsiveness, assurance, empathy and physical appearance of building and staff?

- How do we measure our performance in these areas?

- Do we provide ongoing training to keep all staff conscious of these factors?

- Do we have the right people in management to nurture excellence in customer service? If not, what do we need to do to get them in place?

- Do we have anyone on staff who is chasing families away by confusing efficiency in service with effectiveness in service?

- What is our plan to continue making small, gradual improvements in our customer service delivery?

In short, your goal in writing a service strategy is to analyze your customers, past and present, and plan how best to keep them. Without this kind of careful, conscious planning, you risk failure in years to come.

Pre-Need

Pre-need is in. According to the 2000 Wirthlin Study, 84% of Americans prefer pre-arranging the details of their own funerals over letting others make those decisions. This number is going up year after year; in 1990 it was just 76%.

That's good news for funeral service, right? After all, a bird in the hand is worth two in the bush. The more pre-arrangement business you can capture, the more assured your future, right?

Yes and no. I predict that funeral homes that focus on pre-arrangement dollars over Experience-generated income will fail. If preplanning customers don't feel confident you can create the Experience they envision for the money they're setting aside, they'll increasingly go elsewhere. (Of course, preplanning funds can also be taken to another funeral home after you've closed the deal.) While Boomers may be predisposed to the idea of pre-arranging, they will demand more and more value for the preplanning dollar.

So here's what you do. You make the pre-arrangement process an Experience.

As you know, I believe that funerals are most meaningful and healing when they are personalized. The pre-need process becomes truly valuable—both to pre-arrangers and their survivors—when it, too, is personalized by focusing on the unique lives of those doing the pre-arranging.

What if your pre-need sales presentation focused mainly on gathering personal information about potential pre-arrangers with the chief goal of creating a personalized funeral plan? Salespeople would, in effect, be recording life histories. These life histories could be handwritten or computer-entered in a customer-friendly funeral planning workbook. Once complete, the workbook would not only contain all the pertinent personal data a funeral director needs at the time of death, it would also include sections on important memories, hobbies, significant relationships, music preferences, and more.

As you probably know, the recent U.S. Senate Hearings on "Funeral and Burials: Protecting Consumers from Bad Practices" portrayed pre-need sales practices as "predatory." Almost every pre-need presentation I've seen in my role as funeral service consultant has tried to shame or guilt customers into buying: "You don't want to be a burden on your children, do you?"

Customer service-oriented funeral homes will take the lead in making the pre-planning meeting a positive, meaningful Experience. Customers should come away from the pre-arrangement conference feeling like they've just had their unique life stories honored and that their thoughts and wishes about what has been most dear to them have been recorded. Yes, they've taken care of the financial obligations of their funerals, but they've done so much more than that.

Mark my words: The first company to truly transform the pre-need process into an engaging, memorable Experience will capture the hearts—and pocketbooks—of untold North Americans.

Pricing

Many funeral homes have been over-focused on one product—the casket—and have used upside-down pricing models, building profits into the casket instead of into the creation of personalized ceremonies. Casket stores and e-commerce marketers can sneak under this price umbrella, selling the commodity of the casket for less money, resulting in a perception of better value.

However, if consumers understood that buying from a local funeral home could mean buying an entire, meaningful funeral Experience, they would be less likely to worry about casket prices and more likely to focus on who could best help them honor the person who died.

My observational research suggests that in part, consumers are eliminating the elements of ceremony because they are falling back on a "price averse" purchasing strategy:

PRICE SEEKING: *Paying the most to get the best.* Historically, many funeral service consumers used this strategy.

PRICE AVERSE: *Choosing the lowest price to minimize your immediate cost and risk.* We know that when information, education and choices are lacking, consumers choose whatever costs them the least. The new customer, lacking an understanding of why the elements of ceremony are of value, has shifted toward the use of this purchase strategy.

BEST VALUE: *Choosing the product or service that gives you the best price/value combination.* We know that when information, education and choices increase, consumers move toward this purchase strategy. Common sense tells us that if we can increase their understanding of the value of the elements of ceremony, and truly help them create meaningful funeral Experiences, bereaved families are more likely to make use of this strategy.

The challenge to funeral service, then, is to increase information, education and choices to the consumer. Focus on personalizing funerals. Review your pricing and make sure you aren't "upside-down." Try building your profit into your service fees, not your caskets, urns and burial products—and then make sure you're delivering exceptional service.

Products

Boomers tend not to value the casket—funeral service's traditional profit center. In response to this trend, forward-thinking casket manufacturers like Batesville Casket Company have created complete lines of memorialization, cremation and burial products that can be personalized. When my Aunt Margaret dies, for example, I can buy a pink urn with her favorite flowers depicted on it and an engraved marker with her favorite quote.

Personalization choices like these certainly add value to funeral service products and I encourage you to offer them to families who might find meaning in them.

But thanks to Pine and Gilmore I have another radical thought for you about products. Your products really aren't the casket, the urn, the vault and the headstone. If you're creating memorable Experiences, you must begin to think of your products as the families you serve.

That's right—the customer is the product.

You see, meaningful funeral Experiences change us. After the funeral we are not the same people we were before the funeral. If we have taken part in a personalized funeral Experience, we have begun to meet our six needs of mourning (see Why?), we have paid tribute to the person who died, we have said goodbye in a loving and meaningful way. We have encountered death and we have, through the power of ritual, incorporated its despair as well its hopefulness into our very beings. We have begun to heal.

Such transformations are the most important outcomes of the funeral Experience. Such transformations constitute the true value of what you do. How your customers feel—and are changed—when the funeral Experience is over is the measure of your success.

My customers are my products. My customers are my products. Repeat this mantra the next time a new family walks through your door and see how it changes your attitude and ability to serve them.

Promptness

Anytime you are late in serving a family, you are doing both your company and the family a disservice. Responsiveness, or your funeral home's ability to help families promptly, has a lot to do with whether you convey trust, confidence, and competence to them. Funeral directors with a habit of being late not only hurt themselves but your entire funeral home. As the family waits, they often begin to wonder whether you 1) want to help them and 2) will really be able to help them once you show up.

We know that time can already seem distorted for grieving people. Thirty minutes to a bereaved family will often feel like two hours. Whenever a family expects to be seen at a particular time, the funeral director should be ready at least 15 minutes beforehand and clear his or her schedule so the arriving family will be the one and only priority. The family should feel like you were expecting them and that you are prepared and willing to help.

Another punctuality rule: Never lead a bereaved family down a hall and place them in your "waiting for eternity" room. Put yourself in their shoes and think of how disturbing it is to be made to wait. Now, add the fact that someone you love has just died. How does it feel?

If you have a staff member who is consistently late, sit down with him and immediately discuss the problem. Instead of exploring why he is always late, focus on the need to change his behavior. Request that the behavior change immediately and let him know that you will be monitoring that change. Later on he might benefit from exploring the why of his tardiness (it often has to do with some unconscious need to be perceived as important and busy), but right now insight is not your first goal.

Also, remember that when a short wait is absolutely necessary, people often tolerate it better when they know how long the wait will be. Keep them posted on the length of the delay and don't ignore them in the meantime. Have a staff member wait with them and make them feel comfortable by offering a beverage and responding to any initial questions they might have.

Finally, don't make families that walk in unannounced feel like they aren't welcome. Someone in their life has just died and they want your help. Welcome them with caring compassion and be glad they walked through your doors. I've seen some walk-in families treated as if they were intruders. If anyone on your staff is doing this, they are helping put you out of business! You might benefit from having a staff meeting to discuss staff members' feelings about walk-ins; make certain you have a service strategy that makes everyone feel welcome all the time.

Qualities

From the bereaved families' viewpoint, what makes an effective funeral director? This is not a simple question to answer, for effective funeral directors have philosophies and "ways of being" as varied as those of the people they help.

Having said that defining an effective funeral director is difficult, I must also say this: In my many years as a grief counselor and educator, I have met some wonderful and some not so wonderful funeral directors and I have drawn some broadstroke conclusions about both groups.

Here's my list of effective funeral director qualities. I have designed it to double as a self- assessment tool. As you read through it, I invite you to rate your skills in each area on a scale of 1 (low) to 5 (high). Be honest as you consider both your strengths and your weaknesses. For a more objective assessment, you might also have a friend or colleague rate your skills.

1. **The willingness to adopt a "teach me" attitude.** Effective funeral directors are always learning from those they help. In fact, they realize that bereaved families are the only ones who can teach them about their unique experiences and needs. An effective funeral director sits down with the newly bereaved family and, through a combination of listening and gentle guiding, in effect says, "Teach me what this death has been like for you. Teach me how I can best help you plan and carry out a meaningful funeral ceremony." This "teach me" attitude lets bereaved families know that above all else, you respect their thoughts and feelings.

   For experienced funeral directors, this means setting aside your preconceptions and your "standard" practices. Instead, I challenge you to view each new family in a special light. What are the unique needs of this family? Is a traditional service appropriate for them? If not, what might be? This "clean slate" approach can be draining and time-consuming, I admit, but rigid, cookie-cutter ceremonies are little better than no ceremony at all.

Low   Average   High

1   2   3   4   5

2. The desire and ability to connect with the bereaved family. The effective funeral director takes the time and expends the energy to connect to the newly bereaved family. Effective funerals are personalized. And effective funereal caregiving is personalized, too. You cannot help the newly bereaved family plan a meaningful funeral unless you are physically, emotionally and spiritually present for them in their time of need.

Low   Average   High

1   2   3   4   5

3. The capacity for empathy. Effective funeral directors are empathetic. This means you must develop the capacity to project yourself into the bereaved family's world and to be involved in the emotional suffering inherent in the work of grief. You must strive to understand the meaning of the family's experience instead of imposing meaning on that experience from the outside.

Listening, actively listening, is a critical part of empathy. Actually, listening is a critical component of all the qualities I have listed here. If you listen, the families you serve will tell you—through their words, their gestures, their presence—how you can best help them during this extraordinarily difficult time.

Low   Average   High

1   2   3   4   5

4. The capacity for warmth and caring. To be an effective funeral director, you must strive for a sense of personal closeness, not professional distance, with the families you serve. Though they will not often tell you this, they will be thinking, "Before I care about how much you know, I need to know about how much you care."

Warmth is primarily communicated nonverbally, through facial expressions, posture, gesture and touch. Yes, even touch. While you must assess each individual family's need for and openness to touch, you must also offer your touch when that need makes itself apparent. Remember, however, that touch is culture- and relationship-dependent and that before you can offer physical comfort, you must first establish a relationship with the bereaved family.

As a funeral director, you have an opportunity—a responsibility—to comfort grieving families and to be emotionally available to them.

Low		Average		High
1	2	3	4	5

5. **An understanding of your professional and personal self.** Effective funeral directors understand that their past professional and private experiences with not just funerals but with grief in general affect their work. Actually, you bring the sum total of all your life's experiences to each family you help. You must strive to understand how your background, your strengths and weaknesses, your personal biases—your ways of being—color each funeral you help plan.

Self-awareness is critical to the helping process. I truly believe that you cannot fully understand others unless you have first made the effort to fully understand yourself. Remind yourself each time you sit down with a newly bereaved family that your primary responsibility is to identify their needs and wants and then to help them carry out those needs and wants in the form of a meaningful funeral ceremony. Meaningful for *them*. They need your compassion and gentle guidance, not your insistence on a particular course of action.

Low		Average		High
1	2	3	4	5

6. **The willingness to develop a personal theory of funeral directing.** As a funeral director, you believe your work is important. But it may have been years since you have been asked to articulate why.

Why do you believe funerals are important? What, specifically, constitutes a meaningful funeral ceremony? What do you see as your role in helping bereaved families with the funeral? These are the sorts of questions that, when answered, might go into your own personal philosophy of funerals. While we can borrow and build on the ideas of others, there is tremendous value in challenging ourselves to articulate our own key assumptions about the helping process.

Low		Average		High
1	2	3	4	5

7. **The desire to seek new knowledge about grief and effective funeral direction.** To continue to be effective, the funeral director must be committed to ongoing education. You must take advantage of new resources and training opportunities as they become available. The key, of course, is then to take your new insights and learn to apply them in your work with bereaved families.

Experienced funeral directors also have an opportunity to educate others about the funeral ritual. Perhaps your colleagues would benefit from a regular round-table discussion of their funeral work. Or surely your church or community group would be interested in a talk on meaninful funeral ceremonies. Challenge yourself to plan these types of knowledge-sharing. Of course, each time you meet a new bereaved family you have a responsibility to teach them about the importance of meaningful funeral rituals. This does not mean you must dictate what is best for them, but that you must provide them with the information they need to make sound decisions for themselves.

Low		Average		High
1	2	3	4	5

8. **The capacity to feel personally adequate and to have self-respect.** Helpful funeral directors feel good about themselves. They feel good about their ability to relate to newly bereaved families. Their sense of self-value invites the same self-assuredness in the families they help.

Effective funeral directors never feel superior to those they help, however. They offer their knowledge and experience freely, gladly. They do not talk down to bereaved families and they do not let their time constraints make families feel they are being rushed or neglected.

Low		Average		High
1	2	3	4	5

9. **The ability to recognize and accept one's personal power in the helping relationship.** Tremendous responsibility comes with the helping relationship you have been entrusted with. Because support is so often lacking elsewhere, bereaved families will rely on you—sometimes you alone—to help them through their first days of grief. Do not be frightened by this temporary, heightened dependence on you.

But do not misuse this power, either, You should not feel superior to the families you work with but instead realize that your helping role is to empower them by encouraging their own autonomy and discovery of strengths. Paradoxically, keeping your own personal power under control stimulates the personal power of the bereaved family.

Low		Average		High
1	2	3	4	5

10. **The desire for continued growth, both personally and professionally.** Effective bereavement caregivers continually assess their strengths and weaknesses. They stay in touch with their own losses and how those losses influence and change their lives. In the same way that they encourage the families they work with to grow, they strive to clarify their own values and live by them rather than by the expectations of those around them. They yearn to continue to live and grow each day.

Low		Average		High
1	2	3	4	5

So, how did you do? While there is no acceptable or unacceptable overall "score," I suggest that you examine those areas for which you circled a 1, 2 or even a 3. This is not to say that to be considered good at what you do, you as a funeral director must "score" high in all the above areas. Instead, I urge you to use this list as a personal and professional challenge. Ask yourself, first of all, if you agree that the qualities I have enumerated are useful to effective funeral direction. You might then set a specific course of action for improving your skills where they are weak.

After six months or a year has passed, rerate yourself to check for improvement. If you take this self-assessment seriously, you may find it will help you gain insight into your work with bereaved families, enriching your career and perhaps most important, heightening the profound, healing benefits of a meaningful funeral ceremony for the bereaved people in your care.

Helping the newly bereaved is one of the most draining tasks on earth. But as many of you know, it can offer unparalleled satisfaction. It follows, then, that while becoming a better helper to the newly bereaved is hard work, it, too, is well worth the effort. I challenge you to challenge yourselves and to hone those qualities that make you a better funeral director.

Restrooms

In his book *Customers For Life*, Carl Sewell dedicated an entire chapter to bathrooms. Yes, that's right—bathrooms! I think he has the right idea. Set yourself apart with attractive, well-appointed and, above all, clean restrooms.

Think about it: Most people who visit a funeral home retreat to the restroom at some point during their visit, to use the facilities but also to regroup and "freshen up." Go look at your restrooms right now. Give thought to how you might improve them. They are a true reflection of how you truly value your customers.

Here are some ideas to improve the bathroom Experience at your funeral home:

Make the following available and attractively displayed:
- salon-quality hairspray
- packaged combs
- a hand mirror
- emery boards
- lotions
- perfumes
- feminine napkins and tampons
- clear fingernail polish (for stopping runs in hosiery)
- anti-static/Cling-free spray
- wrapped mints
- mouthwash
- magazines
- tissues

Ideally your restrooms will have a sitting area with upholstered chairs, a mirrored "dressing table" area for freshening up, perhaps a phone for private calls. If you value your youngest customers, you'll also consider installing a small children's toilet and a low handsink in your restrooms. Adults will notice your efforts to serve children and see that you truly care about everyone.

Revitalization

Funeral service has been around for a long time. As any vocation matures, it's easy to forget what its reason for existence was and is.

Think of yourself as just starting out again. You need the families you serve to, in part, tell you what they want. As you listen and learn, you will probably discover they want more personalization and more meaningful Experiences. Your ability to really listen to needs and requests is the driving force behind revitalizing your funeral home.

Ritual Specialist

As you know, many families you serve have no specific religious affiliation. These same families often do not have a clergyperson to whom they naturally turn at a time of death. They often do not find a traditional religious service meaningful to them.

Trends suggest that the number of non-faith families will probably continue to grow. Many Boomers do not attend church on a regular basis and as many as 80% of the X-generation have never been inside the doors of a place of worship.

Are you and your funeral home positioned to effectively meet the needs of this growing number of families? Or do you persist in asking of families with no religious affiliation: "What clergyperson would you like us to call for you?"

I'm certain that if you are reading this book, you agree with the premise that every family you serve is deserving of a personalized, meaningful funeral Experience. If you are upholding the profession of funeral service, you must consciously work to create these meaningful experiences for both religious and non-religious families you are honored to serve.

For many years I have advocated that funeral service have "Ritual Specialists"—lay people and caregivers (this certainly includes interested funeral directors) who are trained to provide meaningful, secular funerals for families who desire them. My colleague and friend Doug Manning (himself a clegyperson) has referred to this concept as "celebrants." Frankly, I don't care what terms we use to describe it, but we need more ritual specialists (celebrants) to meet this most important need.

While not all funeral directors can see themselves in this expanded role (not only planning, but helping facilitate the funeral), for those of you that are interested I encourage you to seek out training and experience. I know that Doug Manning is planning to offer a series of trainings throughout North America. My own Center for Loss offers an annual 4-day retreat learning experience for interested persons, including funeral directors. To learn more about these and other opportunities, simply contact me at the Center for Loss and Life Transition. We must all dedicate ourselves to filling this void and providing meaningful funeral Experiences to each and every family touched by the death of someone precious.

Secular

When a family who hasn't darkened the door of a church in decades comes to you, you may not know how to help. They don't belong to a spiritual community; they're not interested in a religious service or any talk about God; they may well be skeptical of the need for a funeral service period. How do you create exceptional funeral Experiences for non-religious families?

Long-time funeral director Ray Rossell of Pray Funeral Home in Charlotte, Michigan has found a way. Thanks to the efforts of Rossell, Pray now offers a new, personalized and highly innovative style of funeral ceremony. They call it the Family Affirmation Service℠ .

Rossell and a clergy friend got together and decided to develop an informal, participatory service based on the life of the deceased. After all, a life had been lived and it had impacted other people. "Most families see the value in honoring this if they are guided to talk about the life of the deceased," says Rossell.

The Family Affirmation Service often begins with a combination visitation/funeral service, which they call "a gathering of friends." The gathering takes place in a rather informal setting, such as the family's home or a favorite outdoor setting. They also hold Affirmation Services in their visitation room, but they rearrange furniture so the room looks more like a family room in your house. The body may or may not be present. A facilitator, sometimes a clergy member Rossell has helped select or sometimes a layperson the family has chosen, leads those gathered in sharing memories of the person who died. Often music is played and the family may sing a favorite hymn or song. Afterwards the family shares refreshments and talks informally among themselves.

Typically the Family Affirmation Service concludes with a procession and committal service the following day at the burial site. Rossell often leads the brief service at the grave himself.

"We make a concerted effort to personalize both parts of the Affirmation Service as much as possible," says Rossell. "I try to make sure that all the important aspects of the life of the deceased are represented somehow, through music, sharing memories, choice of flowers, memorobilia displays, etc."

Rossell points out that in planning for this type of service, the initial family interview is critical. He sits down with the family and first asks them about the events that led to the death, since this is foremost in their minds. Then he begins to ask them about the life of the deceased.

"For at-need families, there is a tendency to measure the value of a person's life based on the last few weeks, rather than its entirety," Rossell says. "I try to lead the family back to the memories and life events the individual experienced. This takes time and attention. As the family remembers specific accomplishments, anecdotes and activities the deceased enjoyed, they begin to see the value in honoring the life somehow—even if they came to the interview prepared to request direct cremation."

Once the biographical information is gathered, Rossell can see where the family's focus is heading. The next approach, then, is explaining the options that are available, from the tradition-based service to the Family Affirmation Service. Obviously, families will not be aware of the Affirmation Service, so the director has the opportunity to give a full explanation of this option.

If the family chooses to have a Family Affirmation Service, Rossell then helps them choose a facilitator and arranges to meet with the family and the facilitator within the next day, usually at the family's home. He has even created a workbook for this second planning session that helps him and the facilitator give structure to what might otherwise be a somewhat chaotic ceremony. They select an opening, music, often prayer or other readings and a closing to the ceremony. It's also important that the facilitator be prepared to lead the memory-sharing part of the service and know how to skillfully handle stretches of silence, guests who want to share unpleasant memories, etc.

How long does it take to put a Family Affirmation Service together? "I can plan a traditional funeral in one hour," says Rossell. "For a Family Affirmation Service, the initial interview can last 2 1/2-3 hours. The planning meeting with the family and the facilitator can take another 2-3 hours.

"It takes incredible concentration on what the family is saying and feeling. You have to be almost overzealous in learning about the life of the deceased. By the time we're done, though, I'm like part of the family, even if I was a complete stranger to them beforehand.

"Sure, it takes more time. But many families find value in this type of ceremony that they never found in traditional funerals. The reward is afterwards, when families come up to you and say, "I just can't tell you how wonderful that service was and how good it made all of us feel." I've also been told many times, "Wow. That was the best funeral I ever attended."

Rossell can be reached at Pray Funeral Home at (517) 543-2950.

Speeches

As a "gatekeeper of funeral ceremony," I hope you are proud to be a part of funeral service. More than ever before, NOW is the time to let your community know why you do what you do.

A number of factors have contributed to the public's lack of understanding of the funeral's place in our society. To turn this situation around will require public education. Herein lies your challenge as funeral directors. As caregivers, we have both a responsibility and an opportunity to re-educate our communities about the value of funerals.

Of course, you sometimes hear a funeral director say, "People will just think I'm trying to sell them on funerals if I talk about how important ceremony is." My response to that thinking is this: If you don't tell them, who will? I strongly believe it is time for everyone in funeral service to develop a proactive approach to teaching the public about the value of meaningful funerals.

So, how can your individual funeral home contribute to this important educational process? This article explores one of the most important ways your funeral home can contribute to this most important cause—public speaking to community groups.

Speaking to the Public about Funerals

Find someone on your staff who enjoys public speaking. If you don't have a natural choice, hold a staff meeting and try to discover who might be interested in refining their ability to communicate to groups.

Many community groups are always looking for people to provide talks for meetings. Put together a letter or brochure describing the availability of someone from your staff to talk to groups (this is often called a speakers' bureau) about why funerals have been with us since the beginning of time. Provide them with several sample titles of talks you can give. For example:

- "Why I'm Proud To Be A Funeral Director"
- "Creating Meaningful Funeral Ceremonies"
- "Understating the Needs of Mourners"

Encourage them to call your funeral home to schedule a speaker. Get this letter/brochure out to as many potential sources in your service area as possible. You may be surprised by the calls you will get requesting your services. Better yet, when you go out and do a great job, word of mouth spreads and more people will call.

Planning an Exciting Talk

The basics of providing stimulating talks have been with us since Aristotle wrote his book *Rhetoric* twenty-four hundred years ago:

1. Have a central idea or theme,

2. Know your audience, and

3. Divide your talk into a beginning, a middle, and an end.

1. Develop a Central Theme

Before you speak, have in mind a clear theme. Make your language simple and understandable. Speak from your heart, not just your head. Put the ideas you will convey down on paper, and practice, practice, practice! In developing your theme, think of the concept of focus. If you lose focus, you will lose your audience.

2. Determine Who Your Audience Is

Who are the people you will talk to? Every time you speak, make it your business to know who your audience is beforehand.

You are trying to achieve two things with every audience you have the honor of speaking to—understanding and acceptance. You want your ideas to be heard and understood by everyone you speak to. And you want your ideas to be accepted. Otherwise, why would you go to the work to talk to them? To achieve understanding and acceptance, it is vital to know your audience.

How do you learn about your audience? Here is a list of questions to consider using in your preparation:

- What is the purpose of this group? Why do they meet together? (Helps you understand the group you are talking to.)

- How many people will be there? (The smaller the group, the less formal your talk will be.)

- What educational and cultural backgrounds are they? (Be sensitive to these issues.)

- What experience do they have with your topic? (If they are mid-40s and younger, they may not have been to very many funerals.)

- What do they know about you? (How should you be introduced to the group?)

  If you can determine the answers to these questions, you will have met the second basic requirement: know your audience.

3. Creating a Beginning, Middle, and End

A good talk generally has three essential parts—beginning, middle, and end.

The beginning must capture the attention of your audience and introduce your central theme. It must be inspiring enough for the audience to want to listen to the rest.

For example, let's say you are going to talk on "Creating Meaningful Funeral Ceremonies." You might open with the following:

Cultural anthropologist Margaret Mead was very prophetic when years ago she stated, "When people are born, we rejoice, when they marry, we celebrate; yet, when they die, we pretend nothing happened."

Yes, when someone dies in North America we sometime act as if nothing has happened. One of the ways people do that is by questioning if they should participate in a meaningful funeral ceremony. I'm honored to come before you today to explore why meaningful funeral ceremonies are important to all of us.

This kind of beginning makes people want to "lean in" and listen to more of what you have to say.

The middle of your talk presents your ideas in greater depth. It provides information to support your central idea. It must be attractive enough for your audience to want to listen to the rest.

The mid-section of the above presentation might cover the six central needs of funerals that I explore in the book *Creating Meaningful Funeral Experiences.*

1. Acknowledge the reality of the death;

2. Embrace the pain of the loss;

3. Remember the person who died;

4. Develop a new self-identity;

5. Search for meaning; and

6. Receive ongoing support from others.

This kind of mid-section both informs and inspires the audience to think about their own needs when someone they love dies.

An effective ending sums up the central theme and inspires the audience to want to learn more. It provides a powerful close that will really stick in the heads and hearts of your listeners.

For example, the ending for the presentation on "Creating Meaningful Funeral Ceremonies" might be something like the following:

When someone we love dies, we mourn. When we mourn we need the support and love of those who are close to us. The creation of a meaningful funeral is one important way we can let people know we both need and appreciate their support and love at this difficult time.

Thank you for allowing me to talk about how proud I am to be among those who help people who are "bereaved." I remind you that to be bereaved means "to be torn apart" and "to have special needs." When we are torn apart, one special need we have is the creation of a meaningful funeral.

Remember—these three basics are central to a successful talk to members of your community. Some of you are already practicing the principles I've outlined here. If so, congratulations! If not, get going—we must all work together to create value in what we have to offer bereaved families.

Spirit

Do you make time every day to refresh your spirit? All too often the first thing to go when we get so busy is our God-time or Spirit-time. If you get too busy you may risk becoming spirit-less. It seems that God may become easy to forget. I suppose it is fortunate for all us busy people that God is patiently waiting—waiting for us to slow down and have experiences of the divine.

Perhaps one definition of spiritual time is the drawing together of inner and outer experiences and holding them in a center of committed attention. To pay attention to matters of the soul requires that we take time for gratitude, connection, and love. If you have your personal accelerator to the floor constantly, odds are you will suffer from an absence of spiritual time in your daily living.

Every funeral director should have a certain time of the day when he or she doesn't know who died last night, doesn't care how many services will be held today, doesn't need to know who is on-call and who isn't—but he or she does need a time to be present to the spirit of God. If you create this time and space you may at first think nothing is happening. But if you are patient and sit in solitude and stillness something will happen, for the language of the higher power is silence.

Spiritual Time: Five Essentials

1. Establish a Daily Quiet Time

Just as your body needs sleep, so does your mind. Actually, it needs time to be empty, to slow down. Ten minutes a day is an excellent place to start. The key is some amount of dedicated time. A daily quiet time can serve as a boundary between the other parts of your busy life. Making time for solitude also has the advantage of allowing you to see the extraordinary in the ordinary.

2. Seek Spiritual Growth

Go in search of spiritual growth by believing in and reaching out for guidance from whatever higher power conforms to your beliefs. Try regular attendance at a weekly spiritual/religious service that fits with your creed. Join a study group or keep a spiritual journal. Be open to spirituality's imprint on your life.

3. Discover Your Life Mission

"Life Mission" represents the very essence of who you are. It is your deepest intention—the heartbeat, the overall theme that guides your life. Work is a description of what you do, but your life mission is the spiritual perspective of your life, the very meaning of your life. Do you have a sense of your life mission? Are you living out your soul's purpose? Every mission requires commitment and courage. Ask yourself the above questions openly and honestly. If you don't have passion for funeral service, get out!

4. Invest in Prayer Time

Pray for yourself and others and give thanks for all you have received. I like what Mark Twin said about prayer: "I don't know of a single foreign product that enters this country untaxed, except the answer to prayer." Prayer is meeting life at its source, an engagement in active interchange with a higher power. Or, as Simone Weil defined prayer, it is "attention, turning aside to see." If you look for them, you may discover that there are a multitude of things about prayer to see.

5. Stay in Touch With Nature

Recognize that nature has a way of renewing you. Take a walk in the woods, sit by a body of water. Get outside and marvel at nature's gifts.

I've always found profound meaning in the words of Carl Sandburg, who wrote the following:

A man must get away
now and then
to experience loneliness.

Only those who learn how
to live in loneliness
can come to know themselves
and life.

I go out there and walk
and look at the trees and sky.
I listen to the sounds of loneliness.
I sit on a rock or stump
and say to myself

"Who are you Sandburg?
Where have you been,
and where are you going?"

So, I ask you to ask yourself: How do I keep my spirit alive? How do I listen to my heart? How do I appreciate the good, the beautiful and the truthful in life?

Students

What follows is an open letter to funeral service students, written by my friend David McComb of McComb & Sons Funeral Homes in Fort Wayne, Indiana.

So, you have made a decision to become a funeral director. Chances are that you have had some type of funeral service experience by this point in your career. The big question is: What type of experience was it? Did a senior funeral director take time to explain new tasks to you? Or, were you just told to do something you had never done before, with little or no explanation? Were you awake all night answering the phone, or embalming bodies? Did a family member yell at you, or did you have to deal with a mother who just lost her first child? Were you shocked at how little you are being paid for the marathon hours you are working? Would you call your experience to this point positive and meaningful?

There is good news . . . and bad news . . . ahead for you, just as there would be in any other career you might decide to enter. First, the negative. You are going to continue to work long, hard hours, when every other one of your contemporaries is out somewhere having a good time. Unless your father or uncle owns the funeral home where you are working, the pay isn't going to improve much for a long time. The embalming gets a little easier after the first 500 bodies, but it is still a difficult and often thankless task. You are going to be dealing with families at some of the worst points in their lives, and they aren't interested in hearing any of your problems.

But here is the tremendously good news for you. You are joining the ranks of the greatest profession in the world. As you have already learned in your funeral service history class, North American funeral directors have a distinctly proud heritage that spans the last century and a half. Embalmers and undertakers, morticians and funeral service attendants all fulfill daily one of the seven corporal acts of mercy—that of burying the dead. The rewards you will receive as a funeral director can't always be measured in terms of dollars and cents. But when you embalm a body and conduct a funeral and the family can't seem to thank you enough for your work, then you will realize what a wise decision you have made.

Superstars

Do you have someone on your staff who is a "customer service superstar"? This person creates wonderful funerals and the families she works with rave about her. The problem is, she takes a lot of time with families and creates service standards that no one else on the staff can seem to come close to. Other staff members resent her, and quite honestly, so do you.

What do you do?

You wake up and smell the coffee. This "superstar" is the future of funeral service. Celebrate the fact that you have her on your staff. Be glad she takes the time and effort to create exceptional funerals for the families you are privileged to serve. And do not confuse efficiency with effectiveness. I have met way too many funeral directors who are "fast" in making funeral arrangements. Yet, fast usually is not commensurate with the creation of meaningful funerals.

As we all must acknowledge, this is a most interesting and challenging time in funeral service. More and more people are questioning the value of funerals. We need "superstars" who will help teach families the value of creative, personalized and meaningful funerals. To ensure the future of not only your funeral home but the future of funeral service, you need every funeral director performing at his or her personal best, not just doing enough to get services out the door.

Let's give thought for a moment to your ideal funeral director. Construct a 10-point job performance-customer satisfaction scale with the ideal director performing at the top—a 10! Now establish where each of your directors falls on the scale when giving their best effort. Do you have a team of 8s and 9s? That would be pretty good, wouldn't it?

Now, estimate where each of your director's work performance falls on the scale most of the time. Are you still looking at 8s and 9s? Or is it more like 4s and 5s?

The difference between your directors' potential and their usual performance is called the motivation gap.

Your under-performing directors are, in actuality, holding back. Instead of resenting your superstar and trying to bring her down to a 5, why not work to bring your under-performing directors up? Your under-performers may not be doing their best most of the time. Why is that?

Perhaps you don't really expect their best. Instead, you may be trying to bring your superstar down to their level. Excuse me for saying so, but this is foolish!

If you aren't doing everything you can to put value into each funeral and provide excellent service to everyone you serve, you may as well put a big sign up out in the front yard of the funeral home that reads "SLOWLY BUT SURELY GOING OUT OF BUSINESS!"

An additional reason some directors under-perform is that their extra effort isn't appreciated or rewarded, so they hold back.

Both of the reasons I have noted come from a choice the funeral director makes. Most of the time, the choice is made unconsciously. Not many people consciously say to themselves, "I think I'll just do enough to satisfy this family and get through with this funeral." Yet, if you observe some funeral directors you will see this happen, particularly the directors you might rate a 4 or 5 on the scale above.

Becoming a "superstar" funeral director is not simply a matter of skill, it's also a matter of conscious choice. As an employer you have the opportunity to help influence outstanding performance that benefits those you serve, the individual employee, and everyone who hopes to have a future in funeral service.

Surprise!

Funeral homes that create meaningful Experiences for families keep a few nice surprises tucked in their back pockets.

If you listen attentively to a family's needs and then meet those needs, you are providing good customer service. But only when you transcend (another Pine & Gilmore term) those needs do you create truly memorable Experiences. In other words, you must take your customers by surprise.

Many of the examples of personalization discussed in this book would qualify as suprises because they're done so infrequently today. Beacham McDougald's "Life Reflections" video shows (see p. 205) are a touching surprise to funeral home visitors the first time they see one. Placing a casket atop hay bales for a horse lover pleasantly surprised a Wilson & Kratzer family (see Innovation). Calling upon the life and loves of the person who died to personalize the funeral in ways the family might never have imagined creates surprise and thus a memorable Experience.

Try surprising your families with personalized programs. Or a videotape of the funeral. Or a Memory Book filled out by guests at the visitation or funeral service. Or an engraved Memory Box in which to keep memorabilia. Or favorite flowers of the person who died on the anniversary of the death. Or . . . the list could go on and on.

There are hundreds of ways in which you could happily surprise families. The point is to provide welcome yet unexpected touches; instead of telling the family you'll create a lovely wall display with the photos they've provided, surprise them! Of course, you have to be careful that your surprises won't disconcert or overwhelm the family; there can be a fine line between suprising and upsetting when it comes to funeral service. Just be creative and act in the family's best interests and, most often, YOU'll be surprised at how keeping a thing or two a secret really contributes to the Experience.

Symbols

As you work with bereaved families to plan meaningful funeral Experiences, help them understand and draw on the healing power of symbols.

In the funeral ritual, symbols such as the cross (for Christians; other faiths use other symbols), flowers and candles—and of course the dead person's body—provide points of focus for the bereaved. Because they represent such profound beliefs, they also tend to encourage the expression of painful thoughts and feelings. Furthermore, symbols such as these provide the comfort of tradition. Their continuity and timelessness grounds mourners at a time when all seems chaotic.

Symbolic acts, too, often enrich the grief-healing benefits of funerals. When mourners light a candle during the ceremony, for example, they are provided with a physical means of expressing their grief. Planting a memorial tree can be an emotional, physical and spiritual release; this act also creates a "point of mourning" for years to come.

The AIDS quilt and the Vietnam memorial wall are two beautiful, effective mourning symbols for all Americans. What small-scale, personalized symbols or symbolic acts might you be able to help bereaved families create before, during and after the funeral?

Below I have noted a few symbols often used in the context of the funeral ceremony.

Candle flames—spirit; also life's continuation even after death

Cross—faith

Cup—nourishment, abudance, faith

Flowers—support, love, beauty

Mourning clothes—need for support, sadness

Water—source of life

Take a look around your funeral home and note which symbols are displayed and why. Do you use candles (safely displayed and monitored, of course) in the visitation room and chapel? Do you display flower arrangments effectively? Do you have religious symbols available for those families who might like to display them?

The power of symbols is great. Draw on this power in creating exceptional funeral Experiences.

Telephones

Staff member:	Smith Funeral Home
Family member:	My dad just died at the hospital. We need your help.
Staff member:	Well, I'm not a funeral director. Do you need to talk to one?
Family member:	I'm not sure what I need to do.
Staff member:	I'm just part-time here. Maybe you should talk to somebody else.
Family member:	O.K.
Staff member:	Problem is, nobody else is available right now. Do you want me to have somebody call you when they get here?
Family member:	Like I said, I don't know what I need. I need help now!

Often the first part of the Experience people have with your funeral home comes via the telephone. Are your staff members good on the phone? Are they courteous? Prompt in answering and in helping the caller? Compassionate with family members who may be upset about a very recent death?

In the above example, the caller would have a bad impression of Smith Funeral Home right off the bat—an impression that wouldn't fade completely, no matter how well the funeral home might end up serving the family. If I'm in desperate need and I choose to call you for help, I'll never forget it if you're tentative or rude or just plain clueless. When someone loved has just died, that first call to the funeral home is like a drowning person's cry for a life ring: "HELP!" Does your funeral home throw that life ring swiftly and surely, with strength, competence, compassion and the utmost concern for the person in trouble?

Whether you're handling that first at-need phone call or a less pressing call from a customer (or potential customer), good telephone skills are so very important. An interesting thing happens when your staff person picks up the telephone. To the caller, she becomes the funeral home. It doesn't matter to your customers if the person who answers the phone is a part-time student or the owner of the funeral home. The person who answers *is* the funeral home.

With each call that comes into the funeral home, you create an important memory, positive or negative, of your funeral home. How will your funeral home be remembered? Will the caller think, "These people can help me" or "These people really care and are prepared to meet my needs" or, in contrast, "They sure don't sound friendly" or "They don't really seem to want to help me" or "Oh no, another answering service!"

If an effort to create positive phone Experiences, it can be helpful to train staff members in the five primary ways people evaluate your telephone contact with them. These five keys, identified by Dr. Leonard Berry, are the criteria by which potential customers assess you when they come in contact with you. Set aside some meeting time to review these with each of your staff members.

1. RELIABILITY. The ability of your funeral home to provide what is promised, dependably and accurately. Do you always have someone available to answer the phone? If not, do you have a back-up system that forwards calls to you quickly and reliably, day or night?

2. RESPONSIVENESS. The willingness of your funeral home to help families promptly. Do you answer the phone after one or two rings? Does the person who answers the phone put them in touch with someone who can help them right away?

3. ASSURANCE. The knowledge and courtesy you show families, and your ability to convey trust, competence and confidence. When a bereaved family first calls, are you making them feel confident in your funeral home's abilities? Do they hang up feeling that everything will be well taken care of?

4. EMPATHY. The degree of caring and individual attention you show to the families you serve. Are your employees conveying empathy over the phone?

5. TANGIBLES. In the case of telephone customer service, the telephone equipment is the only tangible. Yet it is still a very important criterion. The quality of sound, ease of call transfer, "hold" music, etc. can all dramatically impact your customers' experience of your funeral home.

You can use these five ways people evaluate telephone contact as a springboard to a staff discussion and training on this topic. You may want to have each staff person complete a self-assessment on these five factors. This can generate some excellent discussion and lead to improved telephone skills at your funeral home.

I'd also like to mention the importance of returning phone calls. In funeral service, credibility comes from being someone you can count on. Management consultant Tom Peters has noted that there seem to be two kinds of people in the world: those who return their phone calls and those who don't. Funeral directors who don't return their phone calls promptly and courteously are basically telling families, "I don't really want or need your business."

Ten Freedoms

This list is written for bereaved families. Funeral directors may want to photocopy it and offer it as a handout as they work with families to plan the funeral. It is also available in poster and wallet card form from Companion Press: (970) 226-6050.

Meaningful funerals do not just happen. They are well-thought-out rituals that, at least for a day or two, demand your focus and your time. But the planning needn't be a burden if you keep in mind that the energy you expend now to create a personalized, inclusive ceremony will help you and other mourners in your grief journeys for years to come.

The following list is intended to empower you to create a funeral that will be meaningful to you and your family and friends. Remember—funerals are for the survivors.

1. *You have the right to make use of ritual.*
   The funeral ritual does more than acknowledge the death of someone loved. It helps provide you with the support of caring people. It is a way for you and others who loved the person who died to say, "We mourn this death and we need each other during this painful time." If others tell you that rituals such as these are silly or unnecessary, don't listen.

2. *You have the freedom to plan a funeral that will meet the unique needs of your family.*
   While you may find comfort and meaning in traditional funeral ceremonies, you also have the right to create a ceremony that reflects the unique personality of your family and the person who died. Do not be afraid to add personal touches to even traditional funerals.

3. *You have the freedom to ask friends and family members to be involved in the funeral.*
   For many, funerals are most meaningful when they involve a variety of people who loved the person who died. You might ask others to give a reading, deliver the eulogy, play music or even help plan the funeral.

4. *You have the freedom to view the body before and during the funeral.*
While viewing the body is not appropriate for all cultures and faiths, many people find it helps them acknowledge the reality of the death. It also provides a way to say goodbye to the person who died. There are many benefits to viewings and open casket ceremonies; don't let others tell you this practice is morbid or wrong.

5. *You have the freedom to embrace your pain during the funeral.*
The funeral may be one of the most painful but also the most cathartic moments of your life. Allow yourself to embrace your pain and to express it openly. Do not be ashamed to cry. Find listeners who will accept your feelings no matter what they are.

6. *You have the freedom to plan a funeral that will reflect your spirituality.*
If faith is a part of your life, the funeral is an ideal time for you to uphold and find comfort in that faith. Those with more secular spiritual orientations also have the freedom to plan a ceremony that meets their needs.

7. *You have the freedom to search for meaning before, during and after the funeral.*
When someone loved dies, you may find yourself questioning your faith and the very meaning of life and death. This is natural and in no way wrong. Don't let others dismiss your search for meaning with clichéd responses such as, "It was God's will" or "Think of what you still have to be thankful for."

8. *You have the freedom to make use of memory during the funeral.*
Memories are one of the best legacies that exist after the death of someone loved. You will always remember. Ask your funeral officiant to include memories from many different people in the eulogy. Use a memory board or a memory table. Ask those attending the funeral to share their most special memory of the person who died with you.

9. *You have the freedom to be tolerant of your physical and emotional limits.*
Especially in the days immediately following the death, your feelings of loss and sadness will probably leave you feeling fatigued. Respect what your body and mind are telling you. Get daily rest. Eat balanced meals.

10. *You have the freedom to move toward your grief and heal.*
While the funeral is an event, your grief is not. Reconciling your grief will not happen quickly. Be patient and tolerant with yourself and avoid people who are impatient and intolerant with you, before, during and after the funeral. Neither you nor those around you must forget that the death of someone loved changes your life forever.

Thank Yous

You may be reading the most important piece of "counsel" in this book. The power and value of the hand-written thank you to a family (pre-need or at-need) cannot be overestimated.

Yes, I mean hand-written thank you notes! Families know when you bang out a standard, computerized form letter to them. In today's high-tech world, the appreciation expressed in a hand-written, personal note stands out. The note doesn't have to be long, but it should be personal and express your appreciation for being able to serve the family.

Families do not forget basic kindness during difficult times. I have several funeral director friends who have had family members approach them as much as 20 years after a death, some with tears in their eyes, and thank them for a personalized note.

Now you might say you have a standard practice of telephoning families a week to ten days after the service (or, have an aftercare person who does this). Well, that's great—but making a phone call, or delegating it to someone else is pretty easy. Pick up that pen; writing a note demonstrates a genuine effort to let families know you realize it is an honor to serve them.

You might ask: Whom should the note come from? In my experience, it should come from the person who helped the family arrange and carry out the funeral. If an owner or manager wants to also add a note of appreciation, fine. But, there is no substitute for hearing from the person the family has established the closest relationship with. If that's you, get started writing right now; you will be amazed at how families will respond to you. Oh, and write from your heart, not just your head. Families know who really cares and who doesn't.

Another Oh: If you don't really care, please get out of funeral service ASAP!

Training

You spent weeks looking for just the right employee for a recent job opening. You felt good about the effort you put into interviewing and hiring what seemed to be the best person. Yet, it has been six months since this new employee started and she's not performing up to your expectations—or your customers'. What went wrong?

A good possibility is that the new staff person you hired was not given effective training for the job. Some funeral home managers/owners think that staff training means giving new staff members a tour of the funeral home and reviewing the hours they will be expected to work. Obviously, such cursory introductions don't really qualify as staff training.

If you find yourself thinking the following about staff training, you may be among those who have been ignoring both the obligation and the opportunities that are part and parcel of effective staff training:

1. *My new staff member already has all the skills he needs.* After all, didn't he graduate from mortuary school or work in a similar position in another funeral home? You may take his ability to perform for granted.

   One funeral home manager stated it this way: "We don't need to train. We only hire experienced funeral directors." Yet, service procedures vary regionally and the customer is changing radically. Simply because someone graduated from mortuary school or worked at another funeral home, do not assume he has the knowledge, skills and personality you want in this important position.

2. *No one trained the owner/manager, so why should anyone else need to be trained?* Some funeral home managers have been promoted to their positions of responsibility because they are "good with families." Still, that doesn't mean they ever learned the management skills to train other staff members. In fact, they sometimes believe (and project to others around them), "No one had to train me. I just learned it on the job!" Naturally gifted funeral directors often find it frustrating to watch novices struggle with some aspect of the job that

seems second nature to them. The result: impatience with new staff members who don't instantly perform at high levels.

3. *I've showed him how to do it but he's still not doing it well.* I recently visited a funeral home where the manager was dissatisfied with an employee of 12 months. The concern was that "he isn't good in making funeral arrangements. It takes him four hours to complete each one."

When I observed this staff member, I found him to be very motivated and loyal to the funeral home. He also seemed to enjoy helping families. I asked the manager how much time he had spent training and modeling for the new employee in doing arrangement conferences. The manager responded, "I had him sit in with me two times the first week he was here." It became apparent that this manager did not have an understanding of what it takes to develop skills in the arrangement conference or the patience to train.

And another thing: a four hour arrangement conference may be your best customer service tool, if it's engaging to families and helps them really think out and plan a meaningful funeral experience.

4. *I work in corporate funeral service.* It's the training department's responsibility to train, not mine. What managers who believe this fail to understand is that a training department acts as nothing more than a support system for management. There is no substitute for an initial training period at the actual funeral home where one will work followed by ongoing coaching by senior staff. To delegate training to a training department based outside your individual funeral home is to invite failure.

5. *This person knows what to do.* Some employees will come to you with knowledge about funeral service, but lack skills in delivering those services. I define skill as "the ability to readily and easily utilize knowledge in order to perform." A recent graduate of mortuary school has knowledge, but she will require both initial training and ongoing coaching in the field: the embalmer in the preparation room, the funeral arranger in the arrangement conference, the receptionist in the reception area and on the telephone. The field is wherever the person works. People may bring knowledge to your funeral home, but skills are only developed over time.

Key Principles for Training New Funeral Home Employees

There are several key principles in training new employees in the funeral home setting that can improve their early performance and result in both the employee and the employer being happier with the hiring decision. Among them are the following:

- Those doing the training should themselves be trained in how to effectively train others. If you have someone on your staff who is patient and enjoys teaching, you may have found a great trainer and mentor for new employees.

- Active participation by the new employee is required. Simply telling or showing the new staff member what to do is not enough. The new employee must physically perform some of the activity (under supportive supervision) in order to more fully learn the details. Remember: Mistakes will happen throughout the learning process. Obviously, you will want to work to minimize the impact these mistakes have on the bereaved families you serve. Progress and behavior changes come through increasing strengths.

- The training process should be broken down into small increments so the new employee can achieve early success. This is vital because the reinforcement that comes from achievement is key to the employee's satisfaction and motivation.

- The training/learning climate should be such that the achievement of the intended objective is the new employee's responsibility. This climate includes a clear picture of the end result expected, support from the trainer/manager to get there, and an open line of communication that allows for lots of questions from the new employee.

- The new employee must be motivated if the instruction is to be effective. Screen into your funeral home employees who are open learners, who realize they don't "know it all." Be on the look out in the interviewing process for the arrogant person who already knows how to do everything in funeral service "the right way."

The Ten Basic Steps of Training

1. Review with the new employee the work to be performed.

2. Demonstrate (model) for the new employee the preferred way the work is to be done.

3. Explain the most important parts of the job or task.

4. Demonstrate the most important parts of the job or task.

5. Let the new employee perform the basic elements of the work under the guidance of supportive supervision.

6. Correct and instruct the new employee.

7. Help the new employee do the whole job until a base level of competence is achieved.

8. Provide ongoing coaching for the new employee to be certain no drifting away from the key parts of the job is occurring.

9. Encourage the new employee to ask questions and seek help when needed.

10. Schedule ongoing training opportunities to encourage self-development and reward good work.

Triangle

A funeral director friend of mine recently asked, "Doesn't EVERYTHING work together to focus on the needs of the families we serve?" His question evolved into a discussion of the importance of defining "everything."

As we continued our discussion, I recalled the concept of the "Service Triangle" as described by customer service consultant Karl Albrecht. He provided a frame of reference for "everything" around you. His "service triangle" model emphasizes the role of service systems, service strategies, and service people in any successful organization. I believe it applies nicely to funeral service and helps operationally define the general term "everything."

As you see in the figure below, this model's design is simple but its application is powerful.

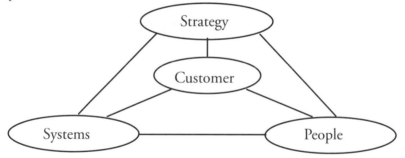

The Service Triangle by Karl Albrecht

As noted in the diagram, each of the four parts interface with each other. Each of the exterior elements—the service strategy, the service systems and the service people—work both separately and together, all the while focusing on the most important member of the service triangle, THE CUSTOMER.

A large body of my recent writings in funeral service education have attempted to motivate funeral home staff to understand that there is a "new customer" out there and that this new customer is the future of funeral service. The service triangle focuses on the critical elements in successfully meeting the needs of your new customers. Your funeral home will need them in place to provide creative, meaningful funeral Experiences for families and to be a value-added organization. Each and every person on staff should be familiar with each of the elements, be able to define their own personal role in the triangle, and most importantly, understand how everyone and everything works together to provide service to the customer—the families you are honored to serve.

Understanding the elements of the service triangle allows the entire staff to make suggestions for improvements in all three areas that surround the customer. The Japanese concept of "kaisan," i.e. small, constant, gradual improvements, can be implemented from the constant feedback from, and communication between, management and frontline employees.

Here's an important reminder: Usually, it's the people in the trenches, the frontline personnel who do the day-to-day work, who are your best source of information to improve service quality. They often know what will work and what won't. Do not leave them out of the loop as you create an overall service strategy. We all know what happened when some of the acquisition companies created strategies and systems without consulting the people in the trenches.

With that in mind, allow me to briefly outline each of the elements of the service triangle and their application to funeral service:

The Service Strategy

Strategy is what your funeral home is all about. This is why you are in business. This tells everyone in the funeral home what is expected of them and how the funeral home plans to deliver value-added service.

The creation of strategy demands careful thought and an understanding of the changing needs of the families you serve. The challenge of this in contemporary funeral service is illustrated by the following: If you work in a funeral home, you are not just in the "funeral business." When your customers come in they aren't just looking for any old traditional funeral. Today's customers are looking for creative, personalized funeral Experiences that meet their unique needs.

You are not just a funeral provider; you are a stager of meaningful, life-commemorating Experiences, a funeral problem-solver, and an advocate for the individual needs of those you serve. Challenge yourself to write out your unique service strategy. Without a specific strategy, you run the risk of lacking focus and mismatching your desires and needs with the desires and needs of your customer.

The Service Systems

The best definition for service systems is "the way you deliver service to your customers." The systems support the staff in everything they do. This is all the little and big things you do to help the families you serve get the products and services they want, in the most efficient and effective manner possible.

The systems—physical, procedural, technical and even mental—help the entire staff provide the best possible service to families. All systems should be focused on making it easier, not harder, to provide excellent service. As the saying goes, "It takes a lot of little things done right along the way to give customers what they want." So ask yourself, "Are the systems you have in place working in ways that both efficiently and effectively serve families?" If not, what changes could be made to make improvements?

The Service People

Service people are just that—the people the funeral home has in place to serve families. This starts with great people who genuinely care about funeral service, who are provided with good training and good tools to do good things. This is about matching people's abilities with the positions they are in.

You can have the best location, the best caskets, state of the art urns, the most affordable pricing structure, and on and on, but these things are meaningless if you have the wrong people working with families. In sum, you need the right people in the right jobs doing the right things. Your best people belong on the frontline working with families to give them value-added customer service.

The Customer

Obviously, there is a reason the customer is in the center position of the triangle. All three of the other elements surround the customer. Yet, never forget customers are the most important. They are why the funeral home exists and they are why jobs exist.

Meeting the needs of today's funeral home customers demands that, among other things, you:

- constantly seek to understand the ever-changing needs and wants of families served.

- give families the Experiences they want, to the best of your ability.

- serve families in as many ways as possible, i.e.. expanding your product and service lines, particularly for cremation options.

- keep families coming back to your funeral home again and again (build loyalty).

- hope that well-served families refer other families in your service area.

Customizing your Funeral Home Service Triangle

Remember—you can create a custom-made service triangle for your funeral home if it includes the following elements: an effective service strategy, customer-friendly systems and customer-powered frontline service providers.

As you review the elements of the service triangle, I warn you not to take for granted that you have them in place and that all is well. As Peter Drucker has reminded us, "Whom the Gods wish to punish, they first grant forty years of business success."

Funeral service has never been so full of challenges, yet opportunities abound. As you make efforts to establish your customized service triangle, you will be better prepared to implement it using the framework outlined above.

Underperforming

Perhaps you have heard of the "Big Lie." This is when the funeral home promises quality services and products but doesn't deliver them. The usual result of the Big Lie is that while this funeral home may serve a family once, it will never serve them again. Through underserving or underperformance, your funeral home will be labeled as one that cannot be trusted and your reputation will spread quickly through the community. The real cost will also come in the repeat service you will lose. As you know, the best funeral home customers are those that return to you again and again over the years.

Underperform on a consistent basis and before you know it you won't be performing at all.

Value-Added

In funeral service workshops I present throughout North America, I sometimes ask participants the following: "How would you define customer satisfaction in the funeral home setting?" As you might expect, I get a variety of definitions:

"Customer satisfaction is when families thank us for a job well done."

"Customer satisfaction is when families participate in a meaningful funeral that helps them receive support from their friends and the larger community."

"Customer satisfaction is when families return to use our services again in the future."

In some ways, each of these answers is correct. All three responses are examples of customer satisfaction. In a more formal way, we can define customer satisfaction as a ratio: It is the relationship between the performance of your funeral home staff and the expectations of the family served. If you exceed their expectations, you have satisfied them. If you under-perform or fall short of their expectations, you leave them feeling dissatisfied.

Perhaps an easy way to remember the above definition of customer satisfaction is with this formula: Customer satisfaction = your staff's performance compared to the customer's expectations. Therefore, value-added service is all about doing something special or going beyond standard service.

If you are in the process of attempting to motivate your entire staff to provide value-added service, you may be meeting with some resistance. "But we already give great service," many funeral home staffers protest. This is what I refer to as "service arrogance," wherein there is a perceived lack of challenge in providing excellent service.

Service is an attitude. It must be delivered by all employees in the funeral home. Value-added customer service is not a spectator sport. You cannot deliver excellent service one time and poor service the next. It must be unceasing, consistent and never yielding to expediency or arrogance.

Those funeral homes that have learned to consistently deliver value-added service have created a strategy for long-term profitability. Service-oriented funeral homes have tended to grow over the years, while product-oriented and poor service funeral homes have declined.

There's another reason you can give your employees for providing value-added service: It's the right thing to do. Families you have the privilege of serving have certain expectations, and your responsibility and opportunity is to exceed those expectations—to give them everything they're looking for and then some.

Without a doubt, focusing on value-added service and converting the philosophy to an overall service strategy is difficult for some. Yet, it is an investment that will yield returns over and over.

So, the next time your employees ask (or imply), "Why should we deliver value-added service?", here are a few responses you might try:

- It's the right thing to do.
- We have a "new customer" out there who is questioning the value of what we have to offer.
- It's the way families deserve to be treated.
- It will probably impact everyone's job security in funeral service.
- We have never had more competition to serve families.
- It makes sense financially.
- It is our objective not just to meet, but to exceed families' expectations.
- And, one more time . . . it's the right thing to do!

I believe that many people in funeral service are aware of how important value-added customer service is. They want to deliver excellent service. They want to do something "special" and go beyond standard service. They want to create exceptional Experiences for families. However, if you discover someone on your staff who consistently teaches you that he doesn't understand the importance of value-added service, he may in fact be teaching you it is time for him to have an "outplacement opportunity."

Value-Added Service Examples: Promising A Lot And Delivering More

Following is a list of examples of value-added service. It might be helpful to sit down as a staff and discuss your perceptions of these examples. You may find you are already doing some of these. You may consider some to be "standard service." You may think that some examples are unrealistic for you to consider offering. Listen carefully to your own and other staff member's perceptions as you discuss this important topic.

- Opening the door for people as they enter or leave the funeral home.

- Offering to handle people's coats for them.

- Providing an easily accesible public telephone for local calls.

- Displaying a vase with flowers in the restrooms as well as tissues, hand lotion and, if space allows, a comfortable chair or sofa.

- Making Tylenol/aspirin available to family members.

- Offering coffee, ice water and other beverages to family members.

- Providing a special, private room for family members to retreat to.

- Designating a special children's area in which they can be noisy or boisterous without disturbing others.

- Offering to go to the family's home instead of having them come to the funeral home to make arrangements.

- Providing a model of a memory table for families as well as many other opportunities for them to personalize the service.

- Going above and beyond the status quo in helping families personalize the service. For example, if a firefighter dies, you suggest placing the casketed body on top of a firetruck in the procession instead of a funeral coach. Or, let's say a family you are serving wants the deceased man's horse to see him one last time to say goodbye. You take the casketed body out under your carport and let the horse have some time with the man's body. (This real example was most appreciated by the family, by the way. As a psychologist, I'm uncertain as to whether it helped the horse or not, but I suspect it did!)

- Placing a courtesy phone call to the family between the arrangement conference and the service to see if they have any questions or need help of any kind.

- Having someone on staff who is trained as a "ritual specialist" who facilitates the service for those families that don't have a clergy person.

- Calling on the family after the service to offer support and determine if there's anything else you can do to help them.

- Being helpful to the general public. For example, if someone calls to ask if you are serving a particular family and you aren't, you respond with a "no" but go on to tell them which funeral home is serving that family and provide them with the phone number.

Not long ago the staff at Watson-King Funeral Home in Rockingham, North Carolina was brainstorming ideas for providing "value-added" customer service. Among the ideas they noted were:

- sending a car to pick up the family
- personalizing memorial folders
- creating a memory table for the family
- providing footstools in the seating area

A Mrs. Johnson had used the services of Watson-King recently. On this particular day, she arrived at the funeral home, by taxi, to pick-up some additional acknowledgment cards.

The funeral director she interacted with (Warren, the manager) happened to note her arrival by taxi and inquired as to why she hadn't driven her car. Mrs. Johnson sheepishly responded that since her husband's death five weeks ago, she had on two occasions left the car lights on, resulting in a dead battery. On both ocassions she had called upon a friendly neighbor who jump-started the car for her.

Yesterday, she had left the lights on for the third time.

Too embarrassed to ask the neighbor for help again, she decided to take the taxi to do a few errands. Having collected her acknowledgment cards, she returned to the waiting taxi for her return home.

For the next few hours, Warren's thoughts kept returning to Mrs. Johnson's predicament. He realized he had a space in his schedule in the late afternoon, and he jumped in his car and drove over to Mrs. Johnson's home.

When he got there he explained to Mrs. Johnson that he had been thinking about her problem and offered to jump-start her car for her. Mrs. Johnson was very thankful. Not only did Warren jump-start her car, he taught Mrs. Johnson how to do it and coached her through the process.

In the weeks following his visit with Mrs. Johnson, Warren and his staff heard many people in the community retell the story of how he had helped "the lady start her car." Apparently, Mrs. Johnson couldn't tell enough people in town how Warren had gone beyond the call of duty.

This true story attests to the power of value-added service. Warren's experience also gives testimony to the fact that service is an attitude and an opportunity. Service is an attitude that says, "I will look for opportunities to exceed the expectations of this unique person or family." Value-added service is, in fact, unique to each person and family you have the honor of serving.

Values

We would probably all agree that the foundation of long-term success for a funeral home is excellent customer service. To provide excellent service requires not only an outward focus on those you serve, but also an inward focus on the core values that guide your funeral home.

Ask yourself: What are this funeral home's values? What do we stand for? What values define this funeral home's culture? Do we project outwardly the internal values we claim to hold up as ours? Is there consistency in our ability to deliver on these values?

Some people mistakenly believe that only large companies have a "corporate culture." Yet, all businesses, large or small, possess values that undergird their everyday interaction with those they serve.

Owners, managers, and employees of funeral homes need to have an awareness of the core values from which they operate. New employees need to be familiarized with these values, so they can live them. When everyone understands the principles your funeral home values, their mission is clear and they come to understand the importance of working together as a team.

Let's explore some potential values that a "customer-friendly funeral home" might aspire to embrace. You might go on to create a mission statement that reflects your funeral home's core values.

Examples of Core Values
(You are encouraged to write out your own.)

INTEGRITY:
We strive to be honest at all times with those we are honored to serve.

GENUINENESS:
We strive to present ourselves sincerely and in non-defensive ways as we provide excellent service.

RESPECT:
We relate to each other as staff and those we serve with respect. This core value involves a receptive attitude that embraces others' feelings, opinions and uniqueness. This mutual respect allows us to serve our customers together—as a team. We practice teamwork and cooperation.

EMPATHY:
We strive to understand people beyond just the factual content of interactions. We are alert to the feelings that loss creates and attempt to be sensitive in all of our interactions.

WARMTH AND CARING:
We strive to provide service in a warm and caring environment. Those we serve should both see and feel this in their interactions with us.

GRATITUDE:
We feel honored and privileged that families have come to us to help them at this difficult time. We have passion for what we do and people sense this in our commitment to help them as best we can.

LEADERSHIP:
As "gatekeepers of the funeral ritual," we play an important role in our community. It is our responsibility to help families create meaningful, personalized funerals and to educate the people of our communities about the value of funerals.

These are but a few core values that a funeral home team might aspire to have and hold. Use this list as a discussion starter for a staff meeting. Work to determine your core values. If you truly want to serve as a team, everyone involved—from the top down—must be committed to your identified core values.

One funeral home I have had the honor to work with, Fairhaven Memorial Park, wrote the following customer value statements. They have even made this text available in brochure form for their customers to take with them.

The Fairhaven Credo

Fairhaven Memorial Park is committed to providing the highest quality of funeral service whether in pre-arrangement or at those times of greatest need. We pledge to provide the finest personal service and facilities for the families we are privileged to serve. Our goal is to make the important difference in the bereavement process of those families.

The Three Steps of Service

1. A Warm and Sincere Greeting. Use the visitor's name if and whenever possible.

2. Anticipation and compliance with visitor needs.

3. Fond Farewell—give them a warm goodbye and use their names if and when possible.

The Fairhaven Essentials

1. The credo will be known, owned and energized by all employees.

2. Smile—"We are on stage." Always maintain positive eye contact. We are never invisible at a service or in the park.

3. Remember, first impressions will make lasting impressions!

4. Be an Ambassador of Fairhaven in and outside of the workplace. Always talk positively; no negative comments.

5. Ues the proper vocabulary. Avoid slang, trite expressions and euphemisms.

6. Create a positive work environment. Practice teamwork and cooperation.

7. Use proper telephone etiquette. Answer within three rings and with a "smile." Ask permission to put the caller on hold. Minimize the number of transfers.

8. The three steps of service shall be practiced by all employees.

9. Instant visitor pacification will be ensured by all. Respond to visitor wishes within 10 minutes of the request. Follow up to ensure satisfaction.

10. Any employee who receives a visitor complaint "owns" the complaint.

11. Communicate visitor comments in writing to fellow employees and management to ensure that our visitors are never forgotten.

12. Escort visitors rather than point out directions to another area of the mortuary or grounds.

13. Be knowledgeable of mortuary and cemetery information, i.e. location, hours of operation, etc.

14. Clothing and uniforms are to be immaculate. Wear proper footwear.

15. Uncompromising levels of cleanliness are the responsibility of every employee.

16. Practice energy conservation and proper maintenance and repair of property and equipment.

17. Ensure all employees know their roles during emergency situations and are aware of procedures.

18. Notify your supervisor immediately of hazards, injuries, equipment or assistance needs you have.

19. Protecting the assets of Fairhaven is the responsibility of every employee.

20. We have only one opportunity to make each service perfect!

Visitation

Here's a powerful equation to remember as you work to create exceptional funeral Experiences for today's families: visitation plus personalization = customer satisfaction.

According to the 2000 Wirthlin Study of American Attitudes Toward Ritualization and Memorialization, 74% of those who had arranged a funeral or cremation for a friend or relative chose to have an open casket for the general public—up significantly from 68% in 1995. That's great news! After all, as you well know, viewing and spending time with the body is a critical step toward reconciling loss for many mourners. (As you know, however, cremation-only customers are less likely to ask for visitation. A recent Options by Batesville study found that 61% of Americans who had arranged a cremation believe there is no need to view the body with cremation.)

Now consider the recent IFFHA survey, which found that 85% of the respondents say that the opportunity to personalize their own or a loved one's funeral is very important. Boomers and X- and Y-geners don't value generic, cookie-cutter funerals; they want truly unique services that befit the unique life of the person who died.

So, most Americans still want visitation. They also want personalization. How can you combine the two in a powerful, cost-effective way that helps families heal? Many of you have routinely begun using memory boards at visitations. Some of you have also used memorobilia tables or displays, showcasing hobby items or other effects of the person who died. These are both excellent, virtually effortless ways to make the visitation more of a meaningful Experience. (I must say, it still amazes me that some funeral homes I visit don't encourage families to make use of these value-added means of personalization.)

Other ideas for enhancing the visitation Experience include:

- Filling the visitation room not with traditional funeral flower arrangements but with vase upon vase of the favorite flower of the person who died.

- Designating a column in the registration book in which guest can write down a special memory.

- Dressing the person who died in his favorite clothing or uniform—not formal wear.

- Suggesting that the family help dress the person who died.

- Playing music that is personally meaningful to the family, or favorite music of the person who died, in the background.

- Holding the visitation somewhere special to the family, perhaps the family garden or the beach. (Of course, you'll have to look into permits and consider other issues for public places.)

- Displaying poster-sized photos of the person who died.

- Playing videotape footage of the person's life or running audiotape in the background.

- Setting up a children's corner in the visitation room with quiet toys, books, and paper and crayons and washable markers so children can, if they wish, create drawings and write messages to place inside the casket.

In talking with Beacham McDougald, a funeral director and good friend of mine from McDougald Funeral Home and Crematorium in Laurinburg, North Carolina, I learned of another surprisingly simple yet highly effective way to personalize the visitation with regular photos. He calls them "Life Reflections" shows and you can create them yourself quite easily with a PC, a scanner and a CD burner.

His "Life Reflections" are simply a collection of photos depicting the life and loves of the person who died. Using a scanner and a piece of software called Corell Presentations, he scans in photos the family brings to him then arranges them in a logical sequence. He runs the Presentation software on a laptop computer which is in turn hooked up to a 36" color TV in a tasteful cabinet (they call it the Presentation Center). The photos are consecutively displayed on the TV screen in a continuous loop throughout the visitation.

Generally, Beacham limits the Life Reflections shows to 40 photos, although he has used many more photos in instances where families wanted them. It takes him about an hour and a half to create a presentation with 40 photos. His wife, Lynn, or Beacham himself scans the photos at 150 pixels per inch, saving them in bitmap format. While they're scanning them in, they take the time to enhance poor quality photos or crop where necessary. The software allows them to do this easily.

In fact, that's one of the main benefits of this medium. Many times families would bring in small or poorly lit photos for their memory boards; this technology blows up photos to the size of a big TV screen, and after they correct for lighting and other flaws, the images look great and are easily viewable.

Once the show is put together, Beacham typically sets each photo to be displayed for 12 seconds before it fades to the next one. He arrived at this number after some trial and error and it seems to work well.

Beacham said that he can also integrate text into the presentations. He can caption the photos or intersperse quotes or other text among the photos. His CD burner also came with software that allows him to create custom CD case covers with a photo, name, birth and death dates of the deceased as well as a label for the CD itself.

But here's the really important question: What do families think of the Life Reflections presentations?

"Last year at this time, only 10-20% of the families we serve accepted our offer to do the Life Reflections show for them, even though we don't charge an additional fee," says Beacham. "This year that number's up to about 75%. In our small community, most people have attended a visitation here and have seen first-hand how the Life Reflections shows work. Now when they come to a arrange a funeral for a loved one, they show up for the arrangement conference with photos in hand. In fact, Life Reflections has transformed the arrangement conference itself. Now, instead of talking about details and filling out paperwork, we end up looking through the stack of photos and talking about the unique life of the person who died. It really makes for a much more personal, interactive arrangement conference."

Beacham adds that the Life Reflections shows also make wonderful, archival-quality keepsakes; he makes them availabe to families after the funeral for just $10 each. (That's where his CD burner comes in handy.) Anyone who has a PC running Windows can just click on the file he's created for them and it will run. It's as easy as that.

For more information on creating Life Reflections-type presentations for your families, contact Beacham at mcdougald@aol.com.

Websites

Does your funeral home have a website? If not, you're missing a great opportunity to improve the Experience you're offering customers.

The World Wide Web is fast becoming a point of entry for millions of consumers. The most recent data shows that more than 120 million Americans are now "active users" of the Internet either from home or at work. When we want to buy a car, we can now start by browsing internet auto sites instead of visiting our local dealer's lot. When we need information on butterflies, we can employ any number of excellent search engines instead of dropping by the library.

And when families in your community need information about funerals and disposition options, they may well look online before phoning you or another funeral care provider. Think of your website as another entrance—and an increasingly popular one at that—into your funeral home. It needs to be just as friendly, just as professional and just as helpful as your staff is when a customer calls or walks in your front door.

But funeral home websites can and should be much more than pretty portals. Computer power now enables even small companies to affordably offer the kind of information, personalization and communication that only amply-staffed corporations once could. Following are some good examples of funeral home websites that are serving customers well.

E-Serving Families with Information

Apart from relatively nominal up-front costs, space on the Web is free, right? If you put your mind to it, your website can provide families with page after page of useful information. A recent study done by Batesville's pre-need division, Forethought, found that consumers think online funeral information "takes the mystery out of funeral planning." Newsletters, articles about grief, pre-need information and forms, maps of your locations, pricing—the list is virtually (pardon the pun) endless. Of course, the goal isn't to overwhelm; be sure to break up information into small, easy-to-read chunks and let readers "click" when they want to read more.

As part of its website, Bradshaw Funeral and Cremation Services (www.brad-shawfuneral.com) of Minneapolis/St. Paul, Minnesota provides a list of Frequently Asked Questions. Visitors can click on "What is embalming and why do it?" and read a brief three-paragraph explanation. They can also learn more about crema-tion, what funeral directors do, what kinds of funeral services are available and much more. How often are you asked similar questions by families in your com-munity? (And conversely, how often might families *want* to ask these questions but are too timid, embarrassed or overwhelmed by grief?) Why not type the answers into your computer and make this kind of empowering information readily and discreetly available to anyone?

In fact, I have had so many requests from funeral homes to post some of my more popular articles on grief on their websites that I created a turnkey website plug-in called "Griefwords" to meet this need. Griefwords contains more than 25 articles such as "Helping Yourself Heal When Someone Loved Dies" and "Helping Children with Funerals" and many more. The plug-in acts as a part of the funeral home's own website, appearing as just another button within the site. When the website visitor clicks on Griefwords, they're provided with a searchable list of arti-cles and complete article texts that can be read online or printed out for hard copy reading. I invite you to check out Griefwords for yourself at www.horanandmc-conaty.com and www.griefwords.com.

Employment opportunity information is available on Newcomer Family Funeral Homes' (www.funeralvalue.com) well-designed website, which serves families in Newcomers' 12 location cities from Arizona to Florida to New York. Based in Wichita, Kansas, Newcomer also provides a concise "Funeral Guide" for at-need families on its website. The guide consists of a checklist of 51 items for families to consider and attend to at the time of a death.

Similarly, Turner and Porter Funeral Directors, Ltd. (www.turnerporter.ca) of Toronto, Ontario includes a helpful button entitled "Funeral Etiquette" on its website, which takes visitors to succinct advice on customs ranging from pallbearer selection to dress to memorial donations.

Forethought's study indicates that consumers find online pricing information especially valuable. In fact, 72% of the study's respondents said they would select a second- or third-choice funeral home that disclosed pricing online over their first-choice funeral home if online pricing wasn't available there.

Horan & McConaty (www.horanandmcconaty.com) of Denver, Colorado has been a leader in this crucial aspect of Web-based funeral information, providing a complete price list on its comprehensive and well-designed website, including descriptions of what each fee includes. I find that many families approach the funeral planning process fearful of costs. Horan & McConaty waylays this fear with clear, forthright pricing on their website for all to see.

Many of the websites I visited in putting together this piece emphasize the importance of the funeral. Gently reminding visitors why we have funerals is a key piece of information that belongs on every funeral home website. You might also consider posting company history, brief funeral director bios, a list of local resources for mourners and links to other grief and death-care sites.

E-Serving Families with Personalization

Another exciting customer service opportunity afforded by the Web is the ability to post personalized tributes to the person who died.

Norris Funeral Home (www.norrisfh.com) of St. Charles, Illinois maintains an online obituary database. Website visitors can scan a list of recent obituaries, clicking on the name of their loved one, or type in the name they're looking for. A complete obituary then appears, including funeral service date, time and location and, when available, a photo of the person who died.

Expanding on this concept, Anderson-McQueen (www.andersonmcqueen.com) of St. Petersburg, Florida hosts an online guestbook. Obituaries are displayed and website visitors can click a button that says, "Sign Memorial Guestbook." The guestbook allows visitors to type in their name, e-mail and mailing addresses and a message. "Share your sympathies, condolences and fondest memories," the instructions invite. Visitors can then print out the entire Memorial Guestbook for the chosen individual.

Canale Tonella Funeral Home (www.canalefuneral.com) of Marquette, Michigan's website proves that sometimes less is more. Their simple but attractive website includes company history and facilities information as well as advice on pre-planning and personalizing the funeral. At the bottom of each page a candle flickers (yes, one of the marvels of the computer age is that an e-candle can really flicker), inviting website visitors to send a memory of the person who died. Instead of posting memorials for everyone to see, Canale Tonella instead passes them along to the family to be read and savored in private.

Other creative online memorial ideas include digital photo albums depicting the life of the person who died—set to background music the family chooses!—and eulogies available for reading online and/or printing out after the funeral service.

E-Serving Families with Interactive Communication

Computers also allow website visitors to participate in other interactive ways in the funeral planning process, thus enhancing their Experience with your funeral home.

Flanner & Buchanan Mortuaries (www.flannerbuchanan.com) of Indianapolis, Indiana is one of many that provides an online preplanning worksheet. Website visitors are presented with a funeral planning form onto which they can enter personal information, military record, funeral service wishes, body disposition requests and other instructions. Then they can either submit this information to Flanner & Buchanan with a click of a button or choose to print it out for their own private use only.

Online sympathy cards are also available at Norris Funeral Home. Visitors simply choose from one of three graphic images and accomanying text, then personalize their e-card with a note. Norris then e-mails the card to the e-mail address provided by the card sender.

Visitors to Anderson-McQueen's website can choose among dozens of flower arrangments and pay for them with the click of a button. Orders are fulfilled by a local florist and cost the same as if ordered directly. Flower buyers enjoy both the convenience of ordering any time of day or night and the peace of mind that the flowers will arrive at the right funeral at the right time.

I've also heard talk of actual funerals being digitally recorded and played in real-time on the Web for out-of-town family members and friends. What a great way to enhance the funeral Experience for the families in your care!

These are just a few of the hundreds of funeral homes across North America that have created customer service-oriented websites. Is yours among them? While I understand the technical and administrative difficulties in creating and maintaining a good website (my own, www.centerforloss.com, has been quite a learning experience), I also understand the value of a good website—both for your company and for your community.

Still, let us not forget that in funeral service, an excellent website does not replace the excellent funeral home. Forethought's study also found that while the majority of consumers are interested in the potential of online funeral planning, 68% still want to meet with a funeral professional face-to-face at some point before finalizing details. By establishing personal contact, consumers said they would feel more at ease and trust that their funeral plan would be honored according to their wishes. In addition, they want to be able to see funeral items they've selected and view the "physical place" where services would be held. (See "A Sense of Place," Chapter 3.) Consumers further indicated that they are not necessarily looking for the lowest price when they search online but rather are interested in finding the best value.

So your website should be another layer of Experience atop the Experience that your staff and facility create—the proverbial icing on the cake. Who wants cake without icing or icing without cake?

Why?

Why do we need funerals? In the day-to-day business of funeral service, it can be easy to lose sight of the "whys" of the important work you do. Here's a refresher.

Essentially, the funeral ritual is a public, traditional and symbolic means of expressing our beliefs, thoughts and feelings about the death of someone loved. Rich in history and rife with symbolism, the funeral ceremony helps us acknowledge the reality of the death, gives testimony to the life of the person who died, encourages the expression of grief in a way consistent with the culture's values, provides support to mourners, allows for the embracing of faith and beliefs about life and death, and offers continuity and hope for the living.

I have discovered that a helpful way to teach about the functions of authentic funeral ceremonies is to frame them up in the context of the "reconciliation needs of mourning"—my twist on what other authors have called the "tasks of mourning." The reconciliation needs of mourning are the six needs that I believe to be the most central to healing in grief. In other words, bereaved people who have these needs met, through their own grief work and through the love and compassion of those around them, are most often able to reconcile their grief and go on to find continued meaning in life and living.

As you read this section, please keep in mind that a meaningful ceremony is but one of many elements that influence a bereaved person's ability to have his or her grief needs met. Obviously, healing in grief is not an event but a process that will unfold for weeks, months and even years after the funeral itself. The funeral is a ritual of ending, but it only marks the beginning of the healing process. Even so, a meaningful funeral can certainly begin to meet all six reconciliation needs, setting the tone for the grief journey to come.

How the funeral Experience helps meet the six reconciliation needs of mourning

Mourning Need #1. Acknowledge the reality of the death.

When someone loved dies, we must openly acknowledge the reality and the finality of the death if we are to move forward with our grief. Typically, we embrace this reality in two phases. First we acknowledge the death with our minds; we are told that someone we loved has died and, intellectually at least, we understand the fact of the death. Over the course of the following days and weeks, and with the gentle understanding of those around us, we begin to acknowledge the reality of the death in our hearts.

Meaningful funeral Experiences can serve as wonderful points of departure for "head understanding" of the death. Intellectually, funerals teach us that someone we loved is now dead, even though up until the funeral we may have denied this fact. When we contact the funeral home, set a time for the service, plan the ceremony, view the body, perhaps even choose clothing and jewelry for the body, we cannot avoid acknowledging that the person has died. When we see the casket being lowered into the ground, we are witness to death's finality.

Mourning Need #2. Move toward the pain of the loss.

As our acknowledgment of the death progresses from what I call "head understanding" to "heart understanding," we begin to embrace the pain of the loss—another need the bereaved must have met if they are to heal. Healthy grief means expressing our painful thoughts and feelings, and healthy funeral Experiences allow us to do just that.

People tend to cry, even sob and wail, at funerals because funerals force us to concentrate on the fact of the death and our feelings, often excruciatingly painful, about that death. For at least an hour or two—longer for mourners who plan the ceremony or attend the visitation—those attending the funeral are not able to intellectualize or distance themselves from the pain of their grief. To their credit, funerals also provide us with an accepted venue for our painful feelings. They are perhaps the only time and place, in fact, during which we as a society condone such openly outward expression of our sadness.

Mourning Need #3. Remember the person who died.

To heal in grief, we must shift our relationship with the person who died from one of physical presence to one of memory. The funeral Experience encourages us to begin this shift, for it provides a natural time and place for us to think about the moments we shared—good and bad—with the person who died. Like no other time before or after the death, the funeral invites us to focus on our past relationship with that one, single person and to share those memories with others.

At traditional funerals, the eulogy attempts to highlight the major events in the life of the deceased and the characteristics that he or she most prominently displayed. This is helpful to mourners, for it tends to prompt more intimate, individualized memories. Later, after the ceremony itself, many mourners will informally share memories of the person who died. This, too, is meaningful. Throughout our grief journeys, the more we are able "tell the story"—of the death itself, of our memories of the person who died—the more likely we will be to reconcile our grief. Moreover, the sharing of memories at the funeral affirms the worth we have placed on the person who died, legitimizing our pain. Often, too, the memories others choose to share with us at the funeral are memories that we have not heard before. This teaches us about the dead person's life apart from ours and allows us glimpses into that life that we may cherish forever.

Mourning Need #4. Develop a new self-identity.

Another primary reconciliation need of mourning is the development of a new self-identity. We are all social beings whose lives are given meaning in relation to the lives of those around us. I am not just Alan Wolfelt, but a son, a brother, a husband, a father, a friend. When someone close to me dies, my self-identity as defined in those ways changes.

Van Gennep, in his book *The Rites of Passage*, emphasized that funerals help mourners with their changed statuses. He pointed out that rites of birth, marriage and death mark separation from an old status, transition into a new status and incorporation into that new status. To use his term, funerals are a "rite of passage." In *The Ritual Process*, Turner reminded us that change in an individual's life is a potential threat to the whole social group, which knows how to treat someone in a clearly defined state but not someone who hovers between states.

The funeral Experience helps us begin this difficult process of developing a new self-identity because it provides a social venue for public acknowledgment of our new roles. If you are a parent of a child and that child dies, the funeral marks the beginning of your life as a former parent (in the physical sense; you will always have that relationship through memory). Others attending the funeral are in effect saying, "We acknowledge your changed identity and we want you to know we still care about you." On the other hand, in situations where there is no funeral, the social group does not know how to relate to the person whose identity has changed and often that person is socially abandoned. In addition, having supportive friends and family around us at the time of the funeral helps us realize we literally still exist. This self-identity issue is illustrated by a comment the bereaved often make: "When he died, I felt like a part of me died, too."

Mourning Need #5. Search for meaning.

When someone loved dies, we naturally question the meaning of life and death. Why did this person die? Why now? Why this way? Why does it have to hurt so much? What happens after death? To heal in grief, we must explore these types of questions if we are to become reconciled to our grief. In fact, we must first ask these "why" questions to decide *why* we should go on living before we can ask ourselves *how* we will go on living. This does not mean we must find definitive answers, only that we need the opportunity to think (and feel) things through.

The funeral Experience provides us with such an opportunity. For those who adhere to a specific religious faith, the meaningful funeral will reinforce that faith and provide comfort. Alternatively, it may prompt us to question our faith, which too can be an enriching process. Whether you agree or disagree with the belief system upheld by a particular funeral service may not matter; what may matter more is that you have held up your heart to that belief system and struggled with the gap.

On a more fundamental level, the funeral reinforces one central fact of our existence: we will die. Like living, dying is a natural and unavoidable process. (We North Americans tend not to acknowledge this.) Thus the funeral helps us search for meaning in the life and death of the person who died as well as in our own lives and impending deaths. Each funeral we attend serves as a sort of dress rehearsal for our own.

Funerals are a way in which we as individuals and as a community convey our beliefs and values about life and death. The very fact of a funeral demonstrates that death is important to us. For the living to go on living as fully and as healthily as possible, this is as it should be.

Mourning Need #6. Receive ongoing support from others.

As we have said, funerals are a public means of expressing our beliefs and feelings about the death of someone loved. In fact, funerals are the public venue for offering support to others and being supported in grief, both at the time of the funeral and into the future. Funerals make a social statement that says, "Come support me." Whether they realize it or not, those who choose not to have a funeral are saying, "Don't come support me."

People often attend funerals not for their own benefit (although they sometimes should examine this rationalization), but for the benefit of the primary mourners. An office worker's daughter is killed in a car accident, and although they didn't know the girl, the office worker's colleagues attend the funeral to demonstrate their support. The mother feels grateful and after her (skimpy) bereavement leave, returns to work hoping her grief will be acknowledged. This public affirmation value of funerals cannot be overemphasized.

Funerals let us physically demonstrate our support, too. Sadly, ours is not a demonstrative society, but at funerals we are "allowed" to embrace, to touch, to comfort. Again, words are inadequate so we nonverbally demonstrate our support. This physical show of support is one of the most important healing aspects of meaningful funeral ceremonies.

Another one is the helping relationships that are established at funerals. Friends often seek out ways in which they can help the primary mourners: May I bring the flowers back to the house? Would you like someone to watch little Susie for a few afternoons this week? I'd like to make a few meals for your family. When might be a good time to bring them over? Friends helping friends and strengthened relationships among the living are invaluable funeral offshoots.

Finally, and most simply, funerals serve as the central gathering place for mourners. When we care about someone who died or his family members, we attend the funeral if at all possible. Our physical presence is our most important show of support for the living. By attending the funeral, we let everyone else there know that they are not alone in their grief.

Words

Have you ever noticed the power of words?

In funeral service, word choices are particularly important. Today's families are leery of the terms "traditional" and "funeral," for example. In response to this trend, some funeral homes are changing their names to include the phrase "Memorial and Tribute Center."

Likewise, the words your staff chooses in talking with a new family are an extremely important part of their Experience, particularly during the arrangement process. Again, the key is to eliminate negative cues and reinforce positive ones as you create a good experience for customers. Here are some words that are definitely negative cues:

A funeral director is asked what he does for a living and he responds, "I work in the funeral *industry*."

The word *industry* denotes something large and impersonal. If you are just "churning out" generic funerals, maybe you perceive yourself as part of an industry. By contrast, if you are continually searching for new and different ways to serve your families, then you are in funeral service. If you are working to upgrade your offerings to the creation of meaningful Experiences, you are in funeral service. If you place greater value on your service fee than on your merchandise fee, then you are in funeral service. In short, when asked, be proud to say you're part of funeral service.

In taking information from a family member, a funeral home staff person inquires: "Where is the *deceased* now?" or, worse yet, "Where are the *remains* now?"

The person has just experienced the death of a family member. He or she is often in shock and hasn't even started to absorb the reality of what the death means. Using terms like *the deceased* is not only impersonal and crude, but it also doesn't assure the family member that the funeral home will carefully take care of the precious body of someone they have loved.

Instead, funeral home staff members should say "your mother" or whatever term best captures the family member's relationship to the person who died.

In arranging the time of the service with the family, the director says, "We have *an opening* at 2:00 p.m."

This terminology makes it sound like your funeral home has to squeeze the family being served in between other appointments. When your schedule is busy, try something like, "Would it be convenient for the service to be held at 2:00 p.m.?" Of course, when you don't have other services scheduled, allow the family to suggest what would be best for them.

A phone call comes to one of four funeral homes in a company. The caller asks if the funeral home is handling so and so's service. The staff member says, "That lady is not at this branch."

Remember — you have funeral homes or chapels, not branches or facilities. A branch is something a bank has. Don't make it sound like you represent a large, impersonal company.

In talking during visitation hours with a family member, a staff person mentions, "We have three other cases in the funeral home right now."

The word cases is impersonal, cold and distant. Instead, refer to other services or families we are serving. A similar example is when a funeral director announces during a clergy breakfast, "I'm sorry but because of our busy caseload, some of our staff couldn't be here." Never use the word caseload. It makes it sound like you work in a factory, not a funeral home that serves families.

When explaining the funeral home's schedule of services to a visiting clergyperson, a staff member says, "We have three calls on the board right now."

"*Calls on the board*" is impersonal and emphasizes the importance of numbers, not people.

"When the phone rings and we are asked to attend to the death of a person, some funeral directors used the term 'death call.' I have always used the phrase 'funeral call' because there is so much more to it than merely a call to move a dead person," says Wendell Hinkson of Bryant-Christians Funeral Home in Kansas.

Wendell's so very right. The words you use behind the scenes affect your attitude about the work you do.

A visitor comes through the door of the funeral home and asks if you have Mr. Jones. The staff person says, "Oh, he's down in number five."

When talking to family members, try not to refer to your visitation rooms just by number. A more appropriate response would be to say, "Yes, let me show you the room," then walk the visitor to the room, making him feel welcome. Better yet, on the way introduce yourself and find out who he or she is. This is not only an opportunity to make guests feel welcome, but to begin to build relationships with them.

In responding to a client's question about how busy the funeral home is, a staff member says, "Well, we do about 300 a year."

It is easy to understand why a layperson would perceive this as an insensitive remark. A preferred response would be, "We are honored to serve around 300 families each year."

Someone calls to learn if you are serving a particular family. The staff person answers, "No, our competitor has that one."

The word competitor is not a word you should use when speaking to the public. Many people don't even understand what you mean when you say it. Instead, if you know who is serving the family, tell them and offer to give directions if necessary. If you don't know, offer to try to find out and call them back.

In talking to a visitor to the funeral home, a staff member says, "We have been working aggressively to increase our marketshare in recent years. We project a 10 percent increase in volume annually over the next five-year-period."

These words, in this context, make you sound like a businessperson who is more concerned about numbers than serving families. Keep these kind of comments behind closed doors.

I would also suggest that everyone in funeral service try to ease up on the use of industry jargon, even when talking behind the scenes with coworkers. That way you won't be as likely to use that language unconsciously when you are speaking with families you serve or the people in your community.

Workshops

In recent years, more and more funeral homes have aspired to become educational resources on grief-related issues in their communities. Why? Not only does it help them better serve bereaved families, it also helps them reach out to the many professional and lay caregivers in the community.

One effective vehicle for educating others about grief is the bereavement workshop. Offered in a variety of formats and topics, the workshop may be a one-day seminar for caregivers on how to support bereaved people or an evening program for the general public. If you have considered offering a workshop in your community, read on. This piece will take you step-by-step through the planning and execution of a successful bereavement workshop.

Why sponsor a workshop?

There are many good reasons to sponsor a bereavement workshop in your community. Perhaps the most important is to help bereaved families and the professionals who care for them, including your staff members. A well-designed workshop is a way for the successful funeral home to thank families served by giving them something of great value—the opportunity to better understand and cope with their grief. Caregivers, including funeral home staffs, appreciate the educational opportunity, too.

Another reason funeral homes sponsor workshops is to mark special events or occasions. A funeral home in Saskatoon, Canada, for example, holds an annual seminar for local caregivers in memory of one of the company's founders. Sometimes funeral homes use a workshop to "kick off" their aftercare programs. And workshops are also a good way for new funeral home owners to establish a renewed emphasis on caregiving in their communities.

Of course, sponsoring a workshop also heightens a funeral home's visibility and promotes a positive public perception. Unlike ads or billboards, bereavement workshops establish the funeral home's reputation as a caring organization while at the same time offering useful information to community members.

Choosing a speaker

Once you've decided to sponsor a bereavement workshop, your next step is to find a good presenter. You may choose to use your own staff and/or local bereavement specialists, but for more impact (and probably a better turnout), you should consider contracting with a leader in the field of bereavement care. A speaker with a national reputation will not only draw more participants, but will also make your workshop seem like a special, "can't miss" event.

If you'd like some help choosing a top-notch bereavement speaker, call your colleagues and local bereavement caregivers. They're sure to provide you with a list of several favorites. You might also find a few names by flipping through your trade journals or calling your national associations.

After you've narrowed down your list to one or two potential speakers, call them for an information packet. This typically includes essential information such as background and credentials, speaking fees, types of programs offered, target audiences, a list of references, and availability. A word to the wise: The presenter's initial response to your query should be both timely and professional. If it's not, consider someone else. All your careful workshop planning will be for naught if your speaker is disorganized or untrustworthy.

If after reviewing the presenter's packet you're confident that he or she will well represent your company, call their references. This is an important but oft-neglected step! Not only will references be able to confirm your choice, but they might also share useful tips about working with this particular presenter or workshop planning in general.

Once your presenter selection is finalized, call him or her to schedule the workshop. At this point most professional speakers will send you a formal letter of agreement that confirms the workshop date, topic, fees, terms of payment and other essentials. Don't be afraid to ask for this kind of written commitment! Without it, you are completely unprotected if the speaker should fail to perform as he or she verbally agreed.

Finding a location

During the days or weeks you are working on selecting a speaker, you should also be working on finding a workshop location. For a number of reasons, we recommend a neutral site such as a hotel. For one, the newly bereaved often find it painful to go back to the funeral home because of its association with the death of someone loved. Moreover, both the bereaved and caregivers will feel less like they are being "marketed to" if the workshop is held somewhere other than the funeral home. Finally, a hotel or conference center can probably host your workshop the most professionally.

Look for a hotel or conference center that can meet all of your workshop needs. Not only will you need meeting rooms and catering, but you will also require audiovisuals and ample parking. Look for flexibility and professionalism, and don't hesitate to compare rates and services at other facilities. Again, confirm your workshop plans in writing with the hotel's contact person.

Promoting your workshop

Location, location and location, they say, are the three most important attributes in real estate. In workshop planning, the key three are promotion, promotion, and promotion!

Workshops don't promote themselves. No matter how well planned, your workshop will be a dismal failure unless the right people receive the right promotional materials at the right time.

We have found that the following promotions timetable works well:

6-9 months before workshop:

Identify the target audience for your workshop and compile the mailing list. In addition to the families you've served, don't forget to comb the phone book and professional association directories for names of caregivers. Professionals at hospices, hospitals, mental health boards, nursing agencies, and school administrations definitely belong on your "must invite" list.

6 months before workshop:

If you haven't done so already, finalize your workshop topic(s) with your speaker. Also, if you plan to offer CEUs to professionals who attend, call a nearby university or the educational department at your local hospital for assistance. Often they'll help you administrate CEU offerings in exchange for being listed as a co-sponsor on the workshop brochure.

3 months before workshop:

Start implementing publicity plans. We've found that a good-looking brochure, which you will send out to your entire mailing list, is the single most important marketing piece for a successful workshop. (Before designing one yourself, see if your presenter has an attractive brochure you can modify for your workshop.) Begin designing posters and ads, if you will be using those, too, and writing press releases.

6 weeks before workshop:

Mail brochures. Send press releases to trade journals, local newspapers, and radio and TV stations. Also confirm your catering and audiovisual needs with your hotel or conference center contact person.

4 weeks before workshop:

Contact your local newspapers and/or radio and TV stations to query their interest in conducting pre-workshop interviews with your presenter. If they bite, this can be an excellent way to get some free publicity. If you are inviting the general public, begin running ads in newspapers. Now is also a good time to compile a handout packet for workshop attendees. Put your presenter's handouts (if he or she has any) in your company pocket folder along with your business card and perhaps your brochure—but try not to feature too many funeral home materials. While it's appropriate to provide a little information about the history and heritage of your funeral home, don't think of the workshop as an opportunity to sell pre-need or other products or services.

2 weeks before workshop:

To encourage their attendance, phone those people you'd especially like to come—key clergy, professionals, lay people—but who haven't yet registered. Confirm travel arrangements with the speaker and make lodging reservations for him or her. Now is also a good time to meet with your contact person at the hotel or conference center to confirm details.

3 days before workshop:

Call in the final number of attendees to the hotel or conference center. Write a brief introduction for your speaker.

Day of workshop:

Sit back, relax and enjoy the fruits of your careful workshop planning!

Post-workshop:

After the workshop is over, don't forget to write thank yous to those people who made it a success. Also don't underestimate the value of post-workshop promotion; press releases detailing the workshop's content and attendance help everyone remember how much they benefited from the event.

Evaluating your workshop's success

One of the best ways to formally evaluate your workshop's success is to design easy-to-complete evaluation forms and distribute them at the end of the presentation. (Or, if you have a handout packet, include the form there.) Most people will fill them out honestly and thoroughly if you ask them to.

You might also consider soliciting written evaluations from those people whose opinions you most value. Almost everyone, you will find, is happy to take the time to offer feedback.

If you have chosen a good speaker and carefully planned and promoted the event, your workshop will likely be a resounding success. Not only will your efforts be rewarded with continued patronage in the weeks and months to come, but you will probably receive immediate gratification in the form of unsolicited letters of thanks from both bereaved people and bereavement caregivers. Here are excerpts from two letters funeral home workshop sponsors recently received:

From a bereaved person:

"Just a note to thank you once again for sponsoring the workshop on Death and Grief. . . (T)his was a very informative and helpful program. Thank you for a profitable and informative time."

From a member of the clergy:

"(The seminar Sudden and Violent Death and Helping Responses) was a real blessing. It helped me in my personal life and in the call upon my life to minister to the hearts of man."

If you'd like the input of funeral homes who have sponsored and organized many successful workshops, please e-mail me: wolfelt@centerforloss.com. I'd be happy to e-mail you a list of Center for Loss contacts. Happy workshopping!

Worktapes

Funeral directors seem particularly prone to work addiction. Many have been influenced by what I call funeral service "worktapes." These worktapes are mostly unconscious messages about work that are stored away in the recesses of the brain. It's as if the mind plays them over and over again, but at a level so deep the conscious mind cannot easily articulate them.

These messages, which are often learned from parents (they often get passed down through the generations in funeral service families), employers and colleagues, can program work behavior. The problem with worktapes is they can threaten one's well-being, leading to exhaustion, frustration and depression.

Below are five common worktapes in funeral service.

Tape #1: Be available at all times.

That's how this business was built, this worktape goes on to say. True, there are times when being available is important and necessary. However, always being available leads to burnout and is not a good practice.

Why? First there are physical and emotional limitations. No one can sanely make three funeral arrangement in the morning, run a funeral in the afternoon, be available at visitation that evening and have a home life.

This worktape forces this type of schedule and increases the risk of having so much energy directed outward that one loses touch with the inner self.

The second reason for turning off this worktape is that is dilutes effectiveness. Focusing a little bit of oneself on everything means committing a great deal to nothing. The result can be polyphasic behavior, which means, at bottom, there's a lot to do but little seems to be accomplished.

This worktape also allows Parkinson's Law to take control: ·Work will expand to fill the time available. Depression, divorce, physical problems, chemical abuse and premature death are all too common among those who become slaves to this mythic worktape.

Tape #2: If you're resting, you're lazy.

What are you doing sitting down? There is always something to do around here. Many people confuse constant activity with productivity. Funeral home management may find it hard to measure an employee's effectiveness. Therefore, activity replaces results as the measure of performance. The busiest bee is thought to be the best worker and is rewarded accordingly.

Yet, some people who look and act busy never seem to accomplish much. Effectiveness must take precedence over busyness.

To maintain physical and emotional health, downtimes in which you pull back and recharge are necessary. Without rest, you're likely not only to lose enthusiasm for work, but also to become exhausted and depressed. As e.e. cummings once noted, "If you can be, be. If not, cheer up and go on about other people's business, doing and undoing unto others until you drop."

Tape #3: To be successful in funeral service, you have to be a joiner.

Many funeral homes mandate that all employees belong to at least three service clubs or other organizations. After all, the reasoning goes, that type of community involvement is what will build a funeral home's business and guarantee each employee's job into the future.

I think it's OK to play this worktape, but only in moderation. Joining and being involved in the community are certainly not bad things. Some over-join—leaving one meeting early to get to another meeting, or committing to an activity only to be too busy to follow through. Joining fever often backfires and leaves others thinking of the joiner as a person who can't be counted on.

Over-joining also ties up evenings with work and club meetings. Family life and friendships suffer. Not only are funeral directors often unavailable for those relationships, they are also unavailable to themselves.

Tape #4: No pain, no gain.

We must under-promise and over-deliver around here. After all, we have to go the extra mile. Referred to by some as the "buckets of sweat syndrome," this myth says that results are directly related to how hard one works.

This worktape can put funeral directors in the mode of constantly working hard to the exclusion of restorative times of rest, play and relaxation. Most successful people work smart, but not always hard. As a savvy someone once said, "When a man tells you he got rich through hard work, ask him, 'Whose?'"

The puritan work ethic may prevent finding fault in this worktape. Many believe that hard work is a sign of an upstanding, righteous person. Many parents taught their children hard work is what won the war and got us out of the Great Depression. How dare we question this work ethic?

Obviously, hard work has its place, but its value is sometimes overstated, and other important criteria for success are ignored. Be on the watch for this "no pain, no gain" philosophy of life. Growing up with this worktape results in an individual with an unusual need to be in control, to achieve perfection, to do what others want and to measure his or her worth by what others think—all common characteristics of the children of workaholics.

Tape #5: If you really care, you'll go beyond the call of duty.

We are here to serve people, this worktape repeats over and over. You have the opportunity to make a difference. If you are truly concerned, you will stay late and come in early.

Be careful about becoming a martyr. Caring and serving others doesn't mean abolishing personal boundaries. Saying no to requests of others now and then will allow time to take care of oneself and one's family.

Moreover, over-dedication to work hours will leave little time to care for family and self. Work must be balanced with the rest of one's life.

Steps to turning off funeral service worktapes

These worktapes often result in work addiction in funeral service. An important step toward having more balance is to consciously hear the worktapes that underlie behavior.

- Slow down and consciously listen to your worktapes.
- Create daily periods of rest and renewal.
- Cultivate and strengthen family and friendship ties.
- Practice setting limits and alleviating stresses you can do something about.
- Develop hobbies and interests outside of work.
- Pamper yourself.
- Develop healthy eating, sleeping and exercise patterns.
- Recognize you are not perfect and that imperfection is OK.
- Seek spiritual renewal and healing.

Obviously, working in funeral service requires not only caring for others, but caring for self. Funeral service worktapes, emotional overload and multiple demands may result in some people questioning why they ever went into funeral service in the first place.

When and if this happens to you, I would encourage you to seek out the support and understanding of a counseling relationship. As a matter of fact, you should be proud of yourself if you care enough about "caring for the caregiver" that you seek out just such a relationship!

Wow

If families leave your care saying, "Wow!", you'll know you've created an exceptional Experience. Michael Yobe of Poteet Funeral Home in Augusta, Georgia tells us of one such occasion:

> An elderly woman passed away when she was living in Texas, though she had been a longtime resident of Pittsburgh. It seems that Texas had quite an influence on her and she became fond of country music, Clint Black in particular. Upon her death, the family called me and we made the necessary arrangements to get her and them back to Pittsburgh for the viewing, funeral mass and burial.

> During the arrangement conference, the family mentioned her fondness for Mr. Black. At the end of the meeting and acting on some unexplained impulse, I went to the local music store and purchased a CD containing her favorite song. Before the funeral mass, family and friends gathered at the funeral home for a prayer before going to church. At the conclusion of the prayer I asked everyone to think of their fondest memories of the deceased while I played her favorite song. This was a total surprise to the family; there was not a dry eye in the place.

> I received many compliments about the personalized service at the committal. Weeks later (after the family discovered the CD with the registration book and flower cards), the family sent the best appreciation letter I ever received along with an invitation to fly to Texas to visit. They will never forget the funeral and I will never forget the feeling I had gotten by providing great service.

Notice how Michael "acted on impulse." His gut and heart were telling him here was an opporunity to do something special, though not difficult, for a family. Listen to your gut. Follow your heart. Be a facilitator, not just a functionary.

Wow.

You

An old but true statement reads, "If you are going to help someone else, the place to start is with yourself." It seems that the more we know and understand about our values, expectations, feelings, and reactions, the more we can understand and appreciate others.

Learning about your own perceptions of the world helps you come to understand others and their unique perceptions. And as you become comfortable with "who you are" others become comfortable being in your presence. In other words, being at ease with yourself helps others feel comfortable in your presence.

This self-growth attitude helps the families you serve trust you. The family will come to know you as a person, not as "Mr. or Mrs. Funeral Director."

To be authentic means to know and be yourself. Some people enter funeral service and discover early in the process that they "do not belong." In my experience this is often, not always, because they cannot be authentically who they are. Maybe they thought funeral directors made tons of money and drove fancy cars. If this is what they valued but couldn't achieve quickly, they left in search of these values elsewhere.

What I'm suggesting is that as we strive to know ourselves, understand ourselves, and accept ourselves, others will sense not only someone who possesses skills, but who has a compassionate presence. If you do not discover this compassionate presence within yourself, you may well want to consider a different profession.

In summary, as you strive to know yourself, you become capable of "being present" with people in pain. You become capable of focusing outside of yourself on the needs of the bereaved family. You also become free to listen, to try to understand as much as possible, to attempt to understand what the family has been through and what they are going through right now.

Overdoing It

Do you ever feel like the girl with the red shoes? The story goes like this . . .

The shoes danced the girl, rather than the other way around...so dance and dance she did. Over the hills and throught the valley, in the rain and in the snow she danced. She danced in the darkest night and through sunrise and she was still dancing at twilight. but it was not good dancing. It was terrible dancing, and there was no rest for her.

We all need personal time away from the high-stress, fast pace of funeral service. We all need time to slow down, go into neutral, to BE instead of DO. Without a doubt, self-care impacts customer care.

If you get so busy doing, you will have no idea where you are going. If you are always "on the run," you won't meet anyone anymore, not even yourself, let alone your family. Personal down-time is one way to stop our red shoes from dancing. Yet, not very often will your fast-paced life invite times of stillness into your life. You will have to cultivate it.

Ask yourself: Do you have a desire to have more peace and balance in your daily life? Do you want this sacred time enough that you will work to create it? What do you need to do to create some time of stillness and quietness in your daily life?

Personal Time: Five Essentials

1. Don't Over-Commit and Under-Perform

Activities and commitments have a way of taking control of your life. The funeral service worktape that says "To be successful in funeral service, you have to be a joiner" puts you at risk for being drained by overcommitment. Learning to say no is not just a good concept—it is necessary. Recognize that it is much harder to stop something than it is to start it. Over-commitment often leads to under-performance. Perhaps as you commit to fewer activities you can concentrate on doing them well, but not apologizing for leaving personal time for you. It was the artist James Whistler who noted that the secret to successful painting was knowing what not to put on the canvas. Likewise, your ability to work smart is dependent upon your deciding what *not* to do.

2. Make Use of Your Prime Time

Attempt to capitalize on your prime time. This is the time of day when you perform best at any given task. Though this isn't always possible in funeral service, when it is possible, you will find you can accomplish more with less effort. For example, if you are a "morning person," try to schedule arrangement conferences prior to lunch. In contrast, if you are less sociable (i.e. a "grouch") in the morning, attempt to schedule arrangement conferences in the afternoon.

3. *Learn to Delegate Effectively*

As you know, carrying out a meaningful funeral experience for families you serve involves staying on top of many details. The art of delegation— assigning to others tasks you want or need to get done— is an essential, learnable skill. Give the job to the person in the funeral home who can do it best. Be certain that the person doing the task has the right training and tools. (For example, some funeral directors are talented embalmers, while other funeral directors could spend days embalming a body and still not do a good job.) Skillful delegation will give you more time to devote to your most important tasks and also provide you with more personal time for renewal.

4. *Build in Time for Play*

The greater the stress you experience at work, the more you need to build in play time. Those people with a compulsion to work all the time actually hinder their own work performance. Play time can rejuvenate you and provide the necessary balance for real success. Most highly successful people have much more to their lives than their jobs.

5. *Disconnect from Technology Now and Then*

Keep in mind that technology is, at times, responsible for our lack of time. Try disconnecting from television, beepers, email, telephones, and faxes for a day, a weekend, or a week. The time you save may be your own!

*ZZZ*zzzzz . . .

Is your funeral home asleep, lulled by the comforting melody of "The Way Things Were," or is it awake to current trends and the possibilities of creating exceptional Experiences for today's families?

Wake up. Smell the proverbial coffee. Rub your eyes and look around you with a fresh objectivity. Do you understand the new customer and what he wants? What types of Experiences are you providing this new customer? Are you integrating all four realms of experience? Have you created a sense of place? Are you reinforcing positive cues and eliminating negative ones? Are you engaging all five senses? Are you charging accordingly for the Experiences you create?

This is an extraordinarily exciting time for funeral service—a time of important change, a time in which you personally can make a lasting difference in thousands of people's lives. I beg you: Don't sleep through it. If you do, you may well wake to the death knell of your own funeral home.

My personal hope for you is that working in funeral service gives substance, meaning and value to your life and that you search for and find meaning in the creation of authentic, personalized funeral Experiences for the families you are privileged to serve.

Send Dr. Wolfelt
Your Customer Service Gems!

Dr. Wolfelt invites you to submit your ideas, practices and actual examples in creating meaningful funeral Experiences for today's families. He may use your ideas in a future edition of this book or as material for an article in *The Director* or *Canadian Funeral News*. Dr. Wolfelt also welcomes customer service questions and challenges.

Please write to Dr. Wolfelt at:

The Center for Loss and Life Transition

3735 Broken Bow Road

Fort Collins, CO 80526

(970) 226-6050

wolfelt@centerforloss.com

Thank you for your participation and your commitment to funeral service.

Bring Dr. Wolfelt
to your community!

One of today's most respected and popular educators, Dr. Alan Wolfelt presents dozens of workshops on grief and funeral service each year to both laypeople and professional bereavement caregivers throughout Noth America. Sponsors include funeral homes, hospices, universities, churches, schools—any organization interested in providing education to community members, area professionals or staff. Presentation formats include all day workshops, breakfast or dinner presentations, keynote addresses and in-house trainings, and range from just a few participants to auditorium-sized audiences. For a free, comprehensive packet on sponsorship opportunities for Dr. Wolfelt, please call the Center for Loss at (970) 226-6050.

"I am writing to acknowledge the profound impact your two workshops have had on our city and our funeral home. We see your two workshops as a turning point in our efforts to be recognized and accepted as part of the professional caregiver community."
Funeral Director/Owner

"Thank you so much for bringing Dr. Wolfelt to our community. He is a wonderful speaker and helped all of us who were fortunate to attend this program."
Bereaved Person

"I am inspired by Dr. Wolfelt's concept of companioning vs. treating the bereaved. Your funeral home is to be commended for making this workshop possible."
Hospice Staff Member

Seminars for Bereavement Caregivers

Have you heard about the great courses for bereavement caregivers taught by Dr. Wolfelt at the Center for Loss in Fort Collins, Colorado? He offers four-day seminars on the following topics:

- *Funeral Service Enrichment Experience*
- *Creating Meaningful Ceremonies*
- *Comprehensive Bereavement Skills Training*
- *Helping Children and Adolescents Cope with Grief*
- *Counseling Skills Fundamentals*
- *Exploring the Spiritual Dimensions of Death, Grief and Mourning*
- *Understanding and Responding to Complicated Mourning*
- *Music, Meditation and Memories*
- *Family Systems Bereavement Care*
- *Support Group Facilitator Training*
- *Companioning Suicide Survivors*

An accredited certification in Death and Grief studies is also available.

For more information, please visit our website (www.centerforloss.com) or call us at (970) 226-6050 to request a course catalog.

Griefwords

Check it out at www.griefwords.com & www.horanandmcconaty.com

The Center for Loss has created a turnkey web outreach program called Griefwords. The program provides a web-based, comprehensive library of articles and book excerpts (25 in all!) about grief for bereaved families and bereavement caregivers.

How does it work?

Griefwords is a website plug-in, not a website. If your website does not already contain a section on bereavement or aftercare, Griefwords will provide you with a complete library of information. If your website contains a section on bereavement or aftercare, Griefwords can become an integral part of the section you have already created.

What's more, our webmaster has designed Griefwords to customize itself to look like part of your website. Your navigation bar, your website colors, etc. will remain when visitors click on the Griefwords link.

Once you've given us your web address and webmaster contact information, we'll simply provide you with a link to the Griefwords plug-in and, with a few keystrokes, the Griefwords library will be part of your website.

How do I subscribe?

To subscribe to Griefwords, please call us or fax us your order by listing Griefwords on the enclosed order form. We'll contact you within 3 business days to get the additional information we need to install the Griefwords plug-in.

Griefwords Web Outreach Program

$350 first year subscription $150/year renewal thereafter

Also by Dr. Alan Wolfelt

Creating Meaningful Funeral Experiences:
A Guide for Caregivers

This revised, updated version of Dr. Wolfelt's groundbreaking *Creating Meaningful Funeral Ceremonies* includes current statistics as well as an introduction to the concept of funerals not just as ceremonies, but as experiences. The book explores the ways in which personalized funerals transform mourners. It also reviews qualities in caregivers that make them effective funeral planners and provides practical ideas for creating authentic, personalized and meaningful funeral experiences.

ISBN 1-879651-38-6 • 80 pages • softcover • $12.95

Companion
PRESS

All Dr. Wolfelt's publications can be ordered from:

COMPANION PRESS

3735 Broken Bow Road
Fort Collins
Colorado 80526
(970) 226-6050
Fax (970) 226-6051

Call for a complete catalog or visit our online bookstore at
www.centerforloss.com

All prices are in U.S. dollars and are subject to change without notice.

Also by Dr. Alan Wolfelt

Creating Meaningful Funeral Ceremonies:
A Guide for Families

This compassionate, friendly workbook affirms the importance of the personalized funeral ritual and helps families create a ceremony that will be both healing and meaningful for years to come. Designed to complement the clergy and funeral director's role in the funeral planning process, *A Guide for Families* walks readers through the many decisions they will make at the time of a death.

ISBN 1-879651-20-3 • 80 pages • softcover • $12.95

Special Set Price: Order both *Creating Meaningful Ceremonies* books for more than 20% off!
Creating Meaningful Funeral Ceremonies set - $20.00

Companion
PRESS

All Dr. Wolfelt's publications can be ordered from:

COMPANION PRESS

3735 Broken Bow Road
Fort Collins
Colorado 80526
(970) 226-6050
Fax (970) 226-6051

Call for a complete catalog or visit our online bookstore at www.centerforloss.com

All prices are in U.S. dollars and are subject to change without notice.

Also by Dr. Alan Wolfelt

Afterwords...
Helping You Heal

A compassionate, affordable aftercare packet for hospices & funeral homes

The distillation of many of Dr.Wolfelt's key teachings, Afterwords offers compassionate, empowering messages about grief and healing to the newly bereaved. Section headings include The Grief Journey, Myths About Grief, Helping Yourself Heal, a Directory of Bereavement Organizations and Support Groups (including websites), a Selected Reading List and the Mourner's Bill of Rights.

Unlike similar packets, Afterwords does not promote its publisher (in this case Companion Press), but instead is designed to highlight your organization's role in after-care delivery. Our name only appears in a brief "about the author" blurb within the text.

Afterwords is an easy-to-use, high quality aftercare packet for hospices, hospitals and funeral homes. And Afterwords is affordable, too. Send for the sample packet for details.

$10.00 (sample packet and ordering information; $10 applied to first order)

Companion
PRESS

All Dr. Wolfelt's publications can be ordered from:

COMPANION PRESS

3735 Broken Bow Road
Fort Collins
Colorado 80526
(970) 226-6050
Fax (970) 226-6051

Call for a complete catalog or visit our online bookstore at
www.centerforloss.com

All prices are in U.S. dollars and are subject to change without notice.